BREAKING

THE

CHAINS

THAT

BIND

YOU

D1522039

BREAKING

THE CHAINS

THAT BIND YOU

A book of understanding the effects of trauma, the importance of healing, and how to transform adversity into purpose.

Mary M Betsworth

DEDICATION

*I wish to dedicate this book in loving memory of
John Bradshaw, one of the most inspiring
writers on emotional health in our time.
Your works and dedication to humanity have
touched and transformed not only my life but
the lives of millions and I deeply and graciously
thank you. I share in your vision and mission
to help others find their authentic self.*

****

*"Reframing my life with my wonder child
helped me to see that everything in my childhood
prepared me for what I'm doing now. The purpose
I found in my meditation was that I am here to
be myself and to proclaim my human freedom
and to help others do the same."*

- John Bradshaw, *Homecoming: Reclaiming and
Healing Your Inner Child*

ACKNOWLEDGMENTS

Thank you to my always supportive husband, Rich, for your support in creating this book. You always hold me in a light that shines brightly with the encouragement, understanding, love, and support I have always desired in a relationship. I learned so much about myself through you. I am glad we finally found each other. You are my rock! And for that and you, I am so very blessed and grateful.

Lisa, my earth angel, and teacher, without you, this journey may not have transpired. Your unconditional love is the motivating force behind me. Your encouragement and guidance changed my life, and for that and editing this book, Mary Marcia, and I are so very grateful. I'm everything I am because you loved me, Lisa.

Marie, thank you for taking the time to read my book and for your inspiring endorsement in the Foreword. We share a sense of commitment to improving the lives of others with our life-learned lessons. May our endeavors benefit and support all those who are ready to discover their authentic selves.

I am so thankful and blessed for my two beautiful children, Lori and Jeff. It was the two of you who first provided me with the unconditional love I was searching for. We have been both teachers and students to one another. I admire your courage to think for yourselves, the caring and generous hearts you each possess, and the uniqueness of who you are. With heart-filled pride, I declare that it has been an honor to be your mother in this lifetime. I love you both to the moon and back a million times.

I was truly privileged for my mother to join me on this life journey. You are the strongest woman I have known. You taught me endurance, tenacity, humor, how to be frugal, and how to have a positive attitude. We grew together in love during our time as mother and daughter. I thank you for being my mother and assisting me in my quest to find love.

To my beautiful daughter in law, Kate, grandchildren and great-grandchildren; I am so grateful that your souls have joined this family. Thank you for your unconditional love. The sound of hearing you call me "Grandma" fills my heart with joy, love, and pride. I feel undoubtedly blessed to have all of you in my life.

CONTENTS

FORWARD

"As a retired licensed social worker, I worked with juvenile rehabilitation, foster parents, and Child Protective Services for 30 years. The contents of this book contain vital information for people of all ages, from teens to grandparents to social workers; as it addresses dilemmas and circumstances that many of us deal with in our lifetime. Numerous mental health and emotional behavioral health conditions are examined. This book will support the young teenager who needs guidance in her/his life because they may be experiencing issues from low self-esteem due to growing up in a dysfunctional home, or from lack of basic care, love, and/or nurturing. Or help a male youth understand why he has a compulsiveness to engage in sexual activities: perhaps he could learn not to choose or pick vulnerable young girls. Mary's book can also help women of all ages who are stuck in a codependent relationship and tolerate emotional and physical abuse. I always believed that emotional abuse has a greater impact on one's life than physical abuse, as bruises fade away, but emotional scars take a lifetime to heal. Mary acknowledges God, spirituality, one's own higher power, and earth angels who play an invaluable part in our lives. She did an amazing job writing this book using her accumulated wisdom from personal experiences and with a lot of research. I wished I had read a book similar to this year's past because I know the information on healthy relationships would have benefitted my personal life.

The author suggests numerous alternative and conventional treatments that are highly effective for healing trauma. There are many quotes in this book by acclaimed individuals that will offer you a new direction of thought. I strongly recommend this book to everyone."

: written by Marie Petersen, Seattle, Washington

■ ■

"I first connected with the author fifteen years ago. Mary Betsworth possesses a kind and supportive nature with a remarkable sense of humor and a unique mind. Her drive and selfless devotion to helping others are amazing.

This book will assist you in recognizing why you have self-sabotaging behaviors. The author provides you with direction on how to achieve healing from trauma and recommendations to manage your recovery and relationships.

As a recovered addict for twenty-nine years, I began my healing by analyzing adolescent trauma that was indicative of having an addiction. Remembering childhood experiences can be painful but necessary to heal and grow, but certainly worth the effort!

Breaking the Chains That Bind You will grace the reader with positive attitudes on life, love, and healing and provide useful tools to heal past trauma. If you are searching for more inner peace, joy, and freedom in your life. this book was written for you."

: written by L. Richard Foster, Omaha, Nebraska

INTRODUCTION

Do you feel indifferent, incomplete, or unsatisfied? Are you searching for fulfillment, purpose, and happiness? To never know love and not discover your true self is living a life without meaning.

Families repeat patterns from one generation to the next that are not always positive. We are all influenced by experiences we may not remember or don't fully understand. Within these pages, you will learn how conditioning and trauma in our formative years affect our lives today and why we believe, feel and act in ways that do not serve us. No one has walked in your shoes, and no one can understand your life but you. If you didn't want something that you got or needed something that you did not receive and it is causing you discomfort, then take the time to explore it. Be honest with your discontent and find the source. Realizing something is missing in your life and maintaining your old views and patterns is not a fun place to be. You alone have the responsibility and power to change.

In these pages, the childhoods of two newsworthy individuals, as well as my own, will be examined, revealing the impact it has had on their adult lives. Readers will learn how to take control of their life, discover accelerated techniques and approaches extracted from neuroscience that will heal childhood burdens, break through emotional barriers of inner shame, overcome dependencies, and heal emotional wounds at their core.

Confronting and healing trauma transforms suffering and opens our hearts to immeasurable peace and joy we never imagined. When negativity is released, only love remains.

This life is not a dress rehearsal. The answers to finding your authentic self are within you. Can you imagine a world in which each of us has accomplished this undertaking? We can change this world, one person at a time, and it begins with you and me. Our journey aims to find wholeness, discover a sense of meaning and purpose in our life, and the love that lies within us. You can only see the light and goodness in others when you first discover it within yourself.

If you want a better life for yourself, are tired of being abused, mistreated, or suffer from addiction, depression, and loneliness, this book was written for you!

CHAPTER 1

A CONDITIONED PATH

*"Finding your life purpose is not about becoming
someone different or chasing after something
better. You align with your true purpose when
you finally recognize your inner being
and accept who you truly are."*
- Anthon St. Maarten

Y our authentic self is who you are genuinely
meant to be. It is living your life according to
your own values rather than someone else's.
Your thoughts, words, and actions are yours and yours
alone, regardless of what others think. Authenticity is
connected to inner peace and happiness, allowing us to
be imperfect and vulnerable. When we live according to
our values, we find more purpose in life, discover our
passions and skills, and fight for the causes we care
about.

By suppressing our true selves, we can feel
lonely, disconnected, and have low self-esteem. We are
afraid people may judge us and hurt our feelings if we
don't go along with the crowd. Being authentic
involves risk. It's easier to be a people pleaser and do
what is expected of us, but by doing so we don't always
feel good about ourselves. When we begin to admit and

understand our strengths and weaknesses; we can filter out what serves our highest good, and what does not.

To know ourselves completely requires self-awareness, insight, and the willingness to unmask our true nature. In childhood, we were programmed with expectations from our parents, teachers, and peers that taught us how to function in life. Early life experiences often define how we see ourselves, others, and the world and make us who we are today. How we act, live, and love is what makes us significantly unique and different from each other. Our perceptions of others are based only on what we see and know. Similarly, as someone else will never fully understand our circumstances, we need to realize that we too, will not understand their circumstances from their perspective. Perhaps your coworker doesn't talk much because her father was an Army officer and did not allow her to speak without permission. Or your annoying aunt (the attention seeker) who constantly complains, was neglected as a child, and no one listened to her. There is no way to know what lies underneath. There is a reason for every decision.

Studies show many psychological and social benefits of being true to your personality, spirit, and beliefs. Those benefits include higher self-esteem, better health, and well-being, successful relationships, and better work performance. Running on automatic pilot in life leaves us feeling lost with no identity and blinds us to our true path in life.

Even if we are not aware, our experiences in childhood affect our personality and behaviors in our adult lives. We try to fulfill childhood desires as adults in a way that is acceptable to society.

We all know that critical inner voice inside our head that is made up of negative thoughts and beliefs about ourselves and others. Originating in childhood, this negative self-talk is an internal enemy that can affect every aspect of our life. But we can learn to quiet that critical inner voice inside us that tells us we are not good enough or cannot succeed.

In examining family belief systems, we can determine where our sabotaging behaviors originated. Exploring our past takes courage and a willingness to look at the sources of our most self-limiting or self-destructive habits. And it isn't necessarily the things that happened to us, but how we interpreted them and how they affected us. When gaining insight into our behaviors, we can consciously make changes to heal our past and accept ourselves as powerful players in our destiny. The impact of childhood experiences has a direct consequence on who you will become in adulthood, and is the foundation on which the rest of our lives are built.

Personal power is essential to finding and becoming our true selves, and creating the world we want to live in. This better world is constructed by shifting our perceptions and rejecting the role of being a victim. We are not defined by the family we were born into. As adults, it is possible to seek out those who make us happy, inspire and support us. Creating this kind of new family can profoundly affect us when surrounded by a support system that encourages and believes in us.

As we share out stories that shape our lives, we connect at a deeper level and gain awareness and understanding of ourselves and others.

"Authenticity is the daily practice of letting go of who we think we are supposed to be and embracing who we actually are." - Brene Brown, *The Gifts of Imperfection*

Undoubtedly, all childhoods are unique as no one had a normal childhood. But when children grow up with stable and responsive parents, they thrive and are encouraged to explore and engage safely in their environment. Understanding each person's experience helps us to be more tolerant of our differences.

Let's examine the upbringing of Lisa Marie Montgomery, who was responsible for the murder of Bobbie Jo Stinnett in 2004.

Lisa was born with fetal alcohol syndrome as a result of her alcoholic mother drinking during pregnancy. One of her first sentences was, "Don't spank me. It hurts." Lisa's mother, Judy, repeatedly beat Lisa and her siblings with belts, cords, and hangers and placed them into cold showers. Her mother brutally smashed in the pet dog's head with a shovel in front of the children for punishment. Other forms of abuse included taping mouths shut, pushing them out into the snow naked, and pimping out her daughters to pedophiles.

Social services took Montgomery's half-sister, Diane Mattingly, after a male friend of the girls' mother raped her. Diane was eight, and Lisa was four. When social services did not take Lisa, Diane was so upset at leaving Lisa behind, that she became hysterical and vomited. Diane says that the household was terrifying, with physical, sexual, and psychological abuse being the norm.

At age eleven, Lisa's stepfather, Jack, sexually assaulted her for the first time. Jack was known as a mean drunk. He built a specially constructed room at the back of their trailer where he could beat, rape, and sodomize little Lisa for the next four years. If she resisted, he would use a pillow to smother her face and tell her that he would rape her sister. Once, after slamming her head so hard on the concrete floor, she suffered a traumatic brain injury.

Lisa's mother, Judy allowed handymen like electricians and plumbers to sexually abuse Lisa in exchange for work in the house. Many stated that her mother was manipulative and evil and received joy in hurting others.

Lisa's mother had multiple partners and was married six times. Lisa was prostituted out to older men in her early teens. Her parents told her that this was her way to pay for her room and board. Her sexual torture lasted several hours at a time with numerous men in a day. The rapes took place in every orifice of her body. Lisa began to dissociate and developed complex post-traumatic stress disorder.

There are many reasons children do not tell someone about their abusive experience. Reasons can include that they perceive it as normal; no one would believe them, guilt, embarrassment, or feeling that they will be viewed as dirty and impure. The perpetrator may have threatened to harm them or a family member if they told someone. It could be the child may not want the person to get into trouble, and they feared they would be removed from the home.

But Lisa did tell her cousin and others that men raped, sodomized, and even urinated on her, but no one intervened. The cousin, a sheriff's deputy, confessed in court that he knew of the abuse and did nothing wrong by not reporting it.

There are many reasons people do not report child abuse and neglect. Either they don't want to get involved, feel it's none of their business, think the child is overreacting, or fear not remaining anonymous. Denial of the issue is easier than getting involved.

The family was living in an isolated trailer home with no running water. Lisa went to school dirty and her clothing was full of holes. She was placed in a special needs class. School administrators suspected abuse in the home but took no steps to investigate or report it.

At age eighteen, most Lisa was forced to marry her younger stepbrother, who continued the cycle of abuse, rape, and beatings. She lived in poverty and was unable to care for the four children she had in five years. Her children, family, and friends noticed Lisa slipping into a world of her own. Her mental illnesses included bipolar disorder, complex post-traumatic stress disorder, dissociative disorder, and traumatic brain injury. She had been sterilized after the fourth baby was born. Lisa was so out of touch that she often did not respond to her name, let alone take care of her children properly. On one occasion, she mistook ammonia for vinegar while cooking. At age thirty-four and living in poverty, she had moved sixty-one times, was divorced, and remarried. And then the behaviors became even more unpredictable.

On December 16, 2004, two days before her crime, her abusive former husband filed for custody of two of their children. She told her new husband that she was pregnant. He knew this was untrue because of her sterilization. Being a mother was a big part of her identity. The threat of losing her children, combined with years of trauma and severe mental illness, pushed Lisa to the edge. Then the unthinkable happened.

Bobbie Jo Stinnett was twenty-three and eight months pregnant. She met Lisa at dog show events, and they emailed one another periodically. Lisa went to her home, killed her, cut the baby girl from Bobbie's abdomen, took the baby home, cared for her, and pretended this was her child. Her husband turned her into the police the next day. In prison, Lisa required a complex cocktail of psychotropic medications to maintain contact with reality. She accepted responsibility for her crime and expressed deep remorse.

Lisa Montgomery committed a crime that she could never take back, and her actions had tragic consequences for many families. Lisa lived a tortured childhood and was herself a victim of terrible crimes. Her actions were unquestionably linked to her history of trauma, mental illness, and brain damage.

Lisa was a survivor of multiple rapes, child abuse, torture, and domestic violence. Lisa was unable to function as a normal person in adulthood due to years of torture at the hands of caregivers. She suffered from a brain injury and untreated severe mental illness. Hundreds of thousands of advocates had called on President Trump to drop her death sentence to life without parole.

Dr. Katherine Porterfield, a renowned expert on torture and trauma, testified that the impact of Lisa's sexual abuse was *massive* and that her dissociative disorder was one of the most severe cases she had ever seen. Sexual and physical violence was the foundation of Lisa's childhood. Lisa was a victim of relentless child prostitution, incest, and rape. She was tried and found guilty in 2007 and executed by lethal injection on January 13, 2021. She was fifty-two years old. Lisa Montgomery was the first woman in sixty-seven years to be executed by the federal government.

Researchers found that adults with child maltreatment histories have an increased potential for violent behavior in later years. Those abused physically are likely to be arrested for a violent crime, and those who experienced neglect were associated with developmental problems and a greater risk for criminal violence. They see the world as a dark and dangerous place and create enemies, building walls in their relationships.

Donald Trump was the host of the show *The Apprentice* for fifteen seasons. The popularity of this TV series provided him with the notoriety that contributed to his election as President of the United States in 2016. The show featured fourteen to eighteen business people who competed throughout a season, with usually one contestant eliminated per episode. Contestants were split into two groups and required to complete business-related tasks: selling products, raising money for charity, or creating an advertising campaign. The losing corporation attends a boardroom meeting with show host Donald Trump to break down why they lost and determine who contributed the least to the team. The episodes ended with Donald Trump eliminating one contestant from the competition, with the words, "You're fired!"

Trump's first appearance on *The Apprentice* showcased him seated in the back of a black limousine and introducing himself. "My name is Donald Trump," he begins, "and I'm the largest real estate developer in New York." Then he proceeded to list off his investments, including buildings, casinos, a winery, resorts, golf courses, model agencies, and more. He bragged about his skills and how he dug himself out of bankruptcy several times, and rebuilt his companies bigger and stronger than ever. People saw him as an icon and as an image of success. Trump supporters viewed him as someone who could get the job done. He lived in an extravagant penthouse in Trump Tower, owned an estate in Bedford, N.Y., where he claimed only the wealthiest people lived. His constant reminder to his followers was how much he valued loyalty.

Donald Trump's childhood was far from nurturing. Donald's father, Fred Trump, was an extremely ambitious workaholic who worked seven days a week. The attention he paid to his children was letting them watch him work. Donald was ignored by his demanding and iron-fisted father, who all but rejected him when he was barely twelve years old. When he did get his attention, he was constantly yelled at, criticized, or punished. His sister-in-law, Mary Trump, describes Fred as a "high-functioning sociopath."

"I strongly suspect that he had a relationship with his father that accounts for a lot of what he became," states Tony Schwartz. Tony spent hundreds of hours with Trump to ghostwrite his bestselling 1987 book, *The Art of the Deal*. "And his father was a very brutal guy. He was a tough, hard-driving guy who had very, little emotional intelligence to use in today's terms."

The childhood of Donald J. Trump has sparked tremendous psychological interest from his character traits to his emotions and words exhibited in public. His mental health became a question of national security. Millions of people around the country and the globe expressed bafflement at the nature of his personality. His tactics and policies appeared unstable and backward in comparison to long-established democratic practices. Trump distorted the facts and outright lied about everything from crowd size at the inauguration to discussions with foreign heads of state. While President Barack Obama was in office, Trump repeatedly claimed that Obama was not born in the U.S. and was an illegitimate president. The lie became so believed that Obama's White House issued a copy of his birth certificate to counter it.

According to an article in Politico Magazine, *The Men Who Gave Trump His Brutal Worldview* by Michael D'Antonio Michael writes, "Donald's father, Fred Trump was a fiercely ambitious man who worked seven days a week and devoted few waking hours to his role as a parent. Although he pushed his son Donald to prevail in every arena to be a "killer" and a "king" Fred didn't tell the young man how to achieve this destiny. In his life story, the most plausible source for explanations for his motivation was his stern, demanding, and ultimately rejecting father. As Donald Trump told me, his father Fred was "very tough" and "very difficult" and someone who "would never let anything go." He was also the man who all but banished his son when he was barely twelve years old."

Michael also states, "While Fred Trump was busy scheming and manipulating, his son developed into a bullying and out-of-control little boy. As Donald recalled to me, he loved to fight... "all kinds of fights, even physical" and the teachers and administrators at the private school he attended in Queens, New York, couldn't manage him. The situation was quite embarrassing to Donald's father, who was a major benefactor to the school. In exasperation, he abruptly removed his son from the family home, which was a mansion attended by servants, and handed him over to the New York Military Academy in upstate New York. Upon arrival, twelve-year-old Donald was put into uniform and assigned to a tiny cell-like room. His parents had expectations that the discipline he received in the school would positively transform his energy. Part of the academy's routine was competition and hierarchy, with physical abuse carried out by students and supervisors.

Trump biographer Timothy O'Brien, author of *Trump Nation* states, "He said to me that he arrived at the military academy, and for the first time in his life, someone slapped him in the face when he got out of line."

"Donald Trump yelled at his classmates," says Trump biographer Marc Fisher, co-author of *Trump*

Revealed. "He pushed them around … he ruled dormitory life with an iron fist."

"All of us were part of this culture of you beat on kids when they didn't do the right thing," says Trump's former military school classmate Sandy McIntosh.

"He loved it," says Gwenda Blair, author of *The Trumps.* "He loved all that stuff because it was also really competitive. Other kids didn't like him all that much. He wasn't that popular because he was so competitive. But it was an environment that he thrived in. Donald's father's overall message to his children was to compete, win, and be a killer. Do what you have to do to win. It was a very different message to the boys than to the girls," Blair says.

Sources describe Trump's time in military school as a five-year lesson in bullying and lessons on how to dominate leading by force and ridicule. Michael D'Antonio, author of *Never Enough.* Michael goes on to say, "Trump's basic philosophy of living, instilled by his fiercely ambitious, workaholic father, enforced by the tough-as-nails coach at his military high school and honed over a lifetime of ruthless deal-making, is fairly simple and severe. Life is mainly combat; the law of the jungle rules; pretty much all that matters is winning or losing, and rules were made to be broken."

Too Much and Never Enough: How My Family Created the World's Most Dangerous Man was written by the president's niece, Mary L. Trump, the daughter of Donald Trump's older brother. Mary states, "Donald Trump was ignored by his father who she describes as a "high-functioning sociopath." When he did receive his father's attention, his father constantly yelled at, criticized, or punished him. Mary claimed that Donald's mother was self-focused and absent, while his father lacked emotion and empathy. "Donald, who was at a very, very critical point in his development as a child, was essentially abandoned by her," says Trump's niece Mary. Donald was age seven when she died.

"To cope," writes Mary, "Donald began to develop powerful but primitive defenses, marked by increasing hostility to others and seeming indifference to his mother's absence and father's neglect. In place of his emotional needs grew a kind of grievance and behaviors including bullying, disrespect, and aggressiveness that served their purpose at the moment but became more problematic over time."

There are many damaging childhood experiences in addition to sexual and physical abuse. Emotional abuse, emotional neglect, living with an addictive or mentally ill parent, having a relative in prison, or witnessing the abuse of a mother or sibling are all damaging. Trauma also includes:

- Bullying
- Racism
- Community violence
- Complex trauma
- Disasters
- Early childhood trauma
- Intimate partner violence
- Medical trauma

The brain itself can't distinguish between types of traumas. It's all trauma. A child's brain has to adapt to survive. When a child is exposed to sudden rage without warning, the stress hormones in the child's brain trigger a fight, or flight response changing the psyche.

"When parents abuse children, the abuse is about the parent's own issues, not the child." - John Bradshaw, *Healing the Shame That Binds You*

In Mary Trump's book, she reveals how trauma is passed from generation to generation. The Trump family considered their lives to be normal and probably never gave a thought to how their behavior was shaped by what they experienced as children. Many people do not know that what they experienced was abuse and thought it was normal. When one becomes aware, they may think, "Wow, this explains my life."

"When you ask Donald about how his mother showed her love, he has nothing to say," says Trump biographer Marc Fisher. Studies show a link between grief, addiction, and mental illness. Losing a parent can lead to increased risks for long-term emotional and mental health issues such as depression and substance abuse. Donald's brother, Freddy, struggled with alcoholism for over twenty years and died at the age of forty-three. According to Mary, Freddy and Donald were both abused by their father, Fred Trump, who favored Donald. She wrote that her grandfather would tell Freddy, "Donald is worth ten of you." Donald tried to win his father's approval all of his life, and his niece stated his traits were dangerous for America.

Mary Trump states, "Child abuse is, in some sense, the experience of too much or not enough.

Donald directly experienced not enough due to his mother's loss of connection at a crucial developmental stage, which was deeply traumatic. Without warning, his needs weren't being met, and his fears and longings went unsoothed. Having been abandoned by his mother for at least a year and having his father fail not only to meet his needs but to make him feel safe, loved, valued, or mirrored. Donald suffered deprivations that would scar him for life. Mary Trump, who has a Ph.D. in psychology, also stated, "Those behaviors hardened into personality traits. No child should go through what happened to him. For those of you who don't like him, I'm not saying you have to feel sorry for him. I'm saying you must understand him. You must understand him so that we don't create more Donald Trumps in this world." In her book, she lists these factors for Donald's abuse.

- "Trump's father emotionally neglected his son when he was a baby and a toddler.

- When Donald Trump was older, his father was emotionally abusive.

- Trump's mother emotionally neglected her son when he was a toddler, at a formative time for his brain development. In other words, he didn't receive the positive experiences necessary for healthy growth.

- Trump watched his father abuse his older brother for years.

- Trump's mother had mental health problems that seemed to have gone undiagnosed and untreated for several years."

"While your childhood is part of you, it doesn't have to dictate who you become." - Psychology Today

Donald Trump has been known to dehumanize women and refer to them as sexual objects. Research shows a link between objectification and aggression towards women. Objectified women are viewed to be less deserving of moral treatment and lack mental abilities to make good decisions. Men who have "Mother Wounds" may feel hollow inside and not know why. Unloving mothers create confusion and lasting wounds in their sons. Without a mother who helps them understand their feelings, they cover up or hide from their emotions. These feelings can be masked by anger.

Katagelasticism is a psychological condition in which a person excessively enjoys laughing at others. People with this condition need to feel unique from others. Degrading out-group members (political preferences, race, intelligence, body types, etc.) or insulting and belittling others can positively impact others' self-worth. Remember, when you insult or criticize someone else, it may say more about how you feel about yourself than the other person. Insecurity over ourselves results in much cruelty in the world and can be observed as bullying.

This man was like no other leader this nation had ever elected, with absolutely no political experience whatsoever, and was impeached twice. He was a businessman with baggage who grew up in a very dysfunctional home. Possessing characteristics of boldness, grandiosity, turbulence, and divisiveness, he was considered dangerous among mental health professionals.

"The mental condition he suffers most from is formally known as a severe instance of narcissistic personality disorder." - Dr. John Zinner, National Institute of Mental Health

Narcissists strive for superiority, are selfish, have a sense of entitlement, a lack of empathy, and a need for admiration. They are constantly searching for someone or something to boost their low self-esteem and feel happy when intentionally making others unhappy. The effects of his narcissistic personality trickled down into society during the first few years of his presidency.

The *Washington Post Fact Checker* began logging President Trump's false or misleading claims from his first day in office to his final day when Joe Biden was sworn in as the country's next president, "Mr. Trump made 30,573 false or misleading claims (from January 10, 2017 to January 10, 2020) which roughly equates to 21 false statements per day." – the *Washington Post.*

Gaslighting is a form of psychological manipulation intended to promote doubt into another's experience of reality. Through contradiction, misdirection, disagreeing, and disallowing, this confuses the other person and causes them to doubt their memory and perception. Trump was good at this manipulation with his frequent lying and consistent effort to disempower others' perceptions of truth.

Greedy people look at the world as if, "It's all about me." Instead of thinking that everyone would benefit as the pie gets larger, they view the pie as wanting to have the biggest piece. They unquestionably believe that they deserve more, even if it comes at someone else's expense. Greedy people are experts in manipulation and control.

Trump did not trust science and questioned his top public health officials' expertise when the COVID-19 epidemic began. He stated the CDC (Center for Disease Control) was lying about the virus to hurt his reelection in November and denied a federal study on masks and the virus.

When the most lethal stage of the pandemic was occurring, he claimed we were rounding the corner. Another time he told us that the virus would "magically disappear." He did not support Dr. Fauci and the suggestions of wearing masks, self-distancing, and washing hands. Dr. Anthony Fauci is an American physician and immunologist and one of the lead members of the Trump administration's White House Coronavirus Task Force. He and the president were at odds with each other, with Trump downplaying the pandemic's severity and attacking his credibility. The president refused to issue a national mask mandate despite contracting the virus himself. During the pandemic, Dr. Fauci was forced to take on security for his family because of Trump supporters' threats.

When Donald J. Trump lost the 2020 election to former vice president Joseph Biden, he claimed he won the election by a landslide even though judges, state and federal elected officials, Republican governors, and the attorney general said he did not. But vast numbers of Americans believed Trump and stood by him. Trump told his supporters to "Have the courage to do the right thing – fight and fight like hell." These very words generated a violent insurrection at the Capitol by his followers, inflamed by his encouragement and lies. Five people died in this event, including a capitol police officer, and dozens more were injured. 638 people have been charged in the Capitol insurrection so far, and seven months after the altercation, more than 570 were arrested for violent acts on Capitol grounds.

Surveys discovered that Trump supporters believed him more than objective sources, even when he was clearly and demonstrably wrong. Deception is cruel and unkind and encourages people to consider information that is not true. A common form of deception is lying and stating something known to be untrue with the intent to deceive. Trust is always essential in all kinds of relationships, from romance and parenting to national government. We assume that most people usually tell the truth. This includes communications and dealings with the media, government, and articles we read.

Trump refused to abide by tradition and concede to the election results and did not call or congratulate Joe Biden. Nor did he participate in ceremonial transfers of power. Trump instead planned and arranged his commemorative departure complete with a red carpet, color guard, military band, and even an 11-gun salute. He was the only president in one hundred and fifty years who did not attend the next president's inauguration or participate in transferring power from one person to another.

The only thing that might be more perplexing than the psychology of Donald Trump is the psychology of his supporters. He fired up the lunatics and the angry. We wonder, what is going on in their brains that makes them so blindly devoted? A big reason would be ignorance. Most were under-informed or misinformed, and they took his word for everything. They were under an illusion and saw him as superior. He wanted to build walls to keep out Muslim and Mexican immigrants and used fear, claiming they were drug dealers, rapists and were a danger to the United States. Remember that Trump was viewed by many as our protector, constantly reminding his followers that he valued loyalty.

Social psychologist Jennifer A. Chatman, the Berkeley Haas leadership expert, states, "Trump's actions were principally devoted to advancing his popularity and power. He said that he is super-smart, a genius. He's established his image as the leader who is cleaning up Washington and is the savior of the common person. He says this so convincingly that none of his supporters are looking beyond that to see that many of the things he's doing are exactly the opposite." This psychological process, called habituation, binds followers to their leader, giving *Trumpism* some qualities of a cult. People are immensely loyal to a cult and feel accountable to its members, and especially to its leader. Connected profoundly to this identity, they fear that defection would let others down or that the group could reject them. When Trump abused his power and was caught frolicking with a porn star, they rationalized supportively and remained passionately loyal. It became more difficult to pull out with each offense, and they would have to question their sanity and mindlessness if they did so.

"Some suggested that generations of creeping economic insecurity have inspired deep anger, compelling many voters in the white middle and working classes to embrace Trump, flaws and all, because he challenges the American status quo." - Berkeley News

"Despite his authoritarian tendencies, President Donald Trump's supporters have stayed with him because of a complex interplay of economic, cultural, and racial factors resulting in a fierce, almost cult-like loyalty," said scholars at the University of California, Berkeley.

I understand this loyalty component when I compare a loyal sports fan staying faithful and steadfast to their favorite team. Being a fan of a particular team feels like being part of a tribe. At our core, like tribal creatures, there is a desire to connect and bond with others. Our subconscious tends to think of them and us. The value in this is that there is a union of togetherness and social connection. Loyalty is seen as a virtue and is an emotional state of mind. Being loyal shows firm and constant support or allegiance to a person, institution, or cause.

Some feared that something would be taken away, such as losing their right to bear arms or reproductive rights. This kind of frustration can turn into anger and rage. Our political views have become more blended into our identities than ever before. Political values are becoming moral values. There are attitudes about what is right and what is wrong. Issues such as immigration, abortion, racial equality, or LGBTQ rights are moral and political issues, and our positions are linked to our identities. An attachment to a particular political side has become more of who we are and not just what we think and makes disagreements feel more personal. Not every Democrat and not every Republican is the same. There are many differences within groups of people, and especially in their cultures.

However, being open-minded is also considered a positive quality. The ability to think critically and rationally is necessary. Open-mindedness is a characteristic that involves being receptive to a wide variety of ideas, arguments, and information. Open-minded people have their own opinions rather than following the crowd. They are not afraid to think for themselves and express their ideas.

Emotionally impaired families and unhealthy behavior rules are passed down from parents to children and have a destructive effect on our society. Adults who refuse to identify and question their source of anger, sadness, and lack of fulfillment in life will continue to live with stress and anger and never discover their authentic selves. Lack of empathy and compassion for others, low self-esteem, anger, narcissism, bullying, dishonesty, guilt, and cold-heartedness are some of the effects of unresolved childhood issues.

The previous examples of childhoods are pretty paramount, but thank God there are children raised in good families. And not all children who suffer abuse or neglect are emotionally affected by it. Many children are raised in homes where there are stable, responsive, caring relationships in the family. When children are encouraged to explore and feel safe in the world around them, they thrive. If we could recognize trauma when it occurs, process it mindfully and emotionally, and realize it is not about us, it would be possible to let it go. But for a child, this isn't easy to do, and unfortunately, it stays in our energy bodies and our unconsciousness. Then we carry these wounds into our adult relationships, careers, happiness, and health.

"Unresolved trauma can take a significant toll on your physical health. Unresolved childhood trauma is particularly insidious, with effects that are gradual and cumulative." - Arielle Schwartz

Even the most loving parents can unintentionally damage a child's self-esteem. The good news is that your genetics does not doom you, and your existence does not have to be a certain way for the rest of your life.

Say goodbye to everything that isn't really you and be who you were truly meant to be.

CHAPTER 2

THE ABSENCE OF
LOVE AND TOUCH

"We first see the world through the eyes of a little child and that "inner child" remains with us throughout our entire lives, no matter how outwardly grown-up and powerful we become. If our vulnerable child was hurt, abandoned, shamed, or neglected, that child's pain, grief, and anger live on within us. I believe that this neglected, wounded inner child of the past is the major source of human misery and the core of all compulsive/addictive behavior."
- John Bradshaw

One in ten adults suffers from some type of mood disorder. Everyone can experience mood swings from time to time, but people with mood disorders live with more persistent and severe symptoms that can disrupt their daily lives. These feelings include ongoing sadness, anxiety, emptiness, hopelessness, low self-esteem, excessive guilt, decreased energy, plus more. Usually, therapy can involve a combination of medications, including antidepressants, and psychotherapy, including talk therapy. I also endorse alternative healing methods such as acupuncture, Emotional Freedom Technique, Yoga, meditation, light therapy, and Reiki, in addition to necessary medications. The most common mood disorders are major and chronic depression, bipolar disorder, and substance-induced mood disorder.

Physical abandonment in childhood can include the loss of one or both parents through death or divorce, being placed for adoption, leaving a child without communication, placement in foster care, or abandoning an infant. This kind of loss runs deep and is exceptionally traumatizing for children. When physically abused, it is challenging for us to form healthy, trusting relationships. Young children are entirely dependent, relying on their parents to meet their physical and emotional needs.

Parents can be physically present but not emotionally available to their children. This happens when there's a lot of stress and chaos in the family, such as violence, verbal abuse, or a parent struggling with addiction or mental illness. Sometimes parents are overwhelmed with other problems like taking care of a sick family member, grief, financial issues, or other major stressors. As a result, the child's needs get ignored.

Attending to a child's emotional needs includes noticing their child's feelings and validating them; showing love, encouragement, and support. Emotional abandonment is about what didn't happen. It's the loss of emotional connection. You may have had a warm place to live, food, clothes, and medicine when you were sick, but your emotional needs may have been ignored. In feeling rejected, children assume they have done something wrong. They feel unworthy of love and attention, and these feelings become internalized as shame, a deep sense of being inadequate and unlovable. There is the belief that they are wrong, bad, unworthy of love, protection, and attention. Thus, abandoned children learn to suppress their feelings, needs, interests, and parts of their personalities to feel acceptable.

"The feeling of being rejected, disapproved of, or conditionally loved by one's primary caregivers is a monumental, long-lasting burden for a child to carry. It produces chronic shame, guilt, and anxiety. The child is blamed for doing something wrong, and in doing so perceives themselves as being bad." - Darius Cikanavicius, *Human Development and Trauma: How Childhood Shapes Us into Who We Are as Adults*

If you were emotionally neglected, it is likely your parents were also emotionally neglected as children. If they never learned how to understand, express, and attend to their own or other people's feelings, they probably repeated the pattern with you because they never learned about the importance of feelings and emotional support. Those of us whose emotional needs weren't met and were deprived of love develop coping mechanisms that disrupt our ability to maintain relationships and affect overall well-being. Coping and defense mechanisms are a way for the mind to cope with stress or disturbing feelings. Defense mechanisms are normal and natural as they reduce anxiety, and every person has them. However, these coping skills can also hold you back from facing reality and prevent you from dealing with an underlying problem or threat.

Denial is one of the most common defense mechanisms. "They're in denial" is a commonly understood phrase meaning someone is avoiding reality. Other strategies include staying busy, satisfying internal needs by helping others; avoiding, projecting our qualities on others; overachieving, disassociating, living in a fantasy, rationalizing, and using humor. Short periods of denial give you time to adjust to distressing situations and alleviate anxiety. However, staying in denial can keep you in addiction and prevent you from seeking help with a problem.

Parents can also put unrealistic expectations on their children. Expecting your child never to get upset, never spill juice, to do everything correctly, and be a straight-A student leaves the child feeling overwhelmed, afraid, inadequate, and exhausted. If you experienced emotional neglect in childhood, you might feel anxious, inadequate, distrustful, and ashamed. These feelings often follow us into adulthood.

Conflict is a natural part of life, but it's harder to do, fearing anger. Conflict demands that we assert ourselves with our feelings and opinions, which can seem incredibly dangerous learning that anger and conflict were unsafe as a child. By befriending and taming our anger, we can deal with conflict in a skillful manner and gain benefits such as proficient communication and inner peace in both our relationships and in the workplace.

Chronic childhood abandonment enforces a belief that the world isn't safe, and people aren't dependable or trustworthy. In adult relationships, you may choose emotionally unavailable partners or friends who abandon or betray you. This unconscious pattern of choosing what's familiar and what we think we deserve is a deep desire to recreate the past with a different outcome proving that we are lovable.

Some become people-pleasers as well as perfectionists. They strive for perfect grades, sports trophies, or other awards to prove they're worthy. They learned that you couldn't make any mistakes, act up, need anything, or express any negative or vulnerable emotions to be accepted and loved. These victims become depressed and anxious and act out their pain by hurting themselves or others, breaking the rules, and numbing their feelings with drugs and alcohol. But nothing can ever fill the hole left by a lack of unconditional love and acceptance from your parents.

Psychology tells us that validation is required if our needs did not get met as a child. Validation is the understanding and confirmation of another person's emotional experience and is a precursor to healing and growth.

I grew up in a home lacking love and tenderness and never hearing "I love you," receiving a hug or hearing praise. I experienced touch only when being spanked or hit in the head with a hairbrush for not being still. Dependent on a mother who informed me that if she did not deliver the spanking, my father would when he came home, which would hurt worse. I constantly sought to be perfect to avoid being struck. Always on edge for fear of doing something wrong, I spent a lot of time alone and sitting in closets to see if anyone would miss me.

My career choices were to become a nun, a teacher, or a taxi driver. Religion was important to me as it afforded me some peace and comfort.

Religion helps us manage our stress and affects our emotional life, therefore, boosting mental health.

I experienced a sudden dissociative flashback in my forties and was transported back into time. I was twelve years old, sitting alone in the bathroom and sobbing as I placed cold wash rags on a swollen, red, inflamed, hand-shaped bruise on my thigh created by my mother. Emotional flashbacks can be triggered by a situation, circumstance, or event that reminds you exactly what happened to you in childhood. You can feel dragged back to those feelings of helplessness and despair.

I find it hard to justify spanking. It teaches your child that violence is acceptable. How can you instruct your child not to hit someone when you are hitting them? Deliberately instilling pain in your child is cruel. Spanking is traumatizing, leaving them with the feeling that something is wrong with them. Spanking creates resentment and self-image problems. It leaves the child feeling insecure, powerless, unworthy, unloved, and disrespected. Crying does not stop. It increases. I cannot find any positive benefits in hitting a child. I am also aware of how easy it is for parents to lose their temper and strike a child generating self-remorse and guilt.

Back then, they called it discipline. A common phrase at that time was "children should be seen and not heard." Then what is a child to do with his natural state of spontaneity and joy? When these natural feelings are repressed, they can later emerge as a pleasure-seeking shadow self.

Disciplining children in that manner is now viewed as harsh, strict, and oppressive. Research shows that spanking may lead to antisocial behavior, aggression, and mental health issues for children. It can also affect normal brain development.

I was a very sensitive and curious child. "What is wrong with you? And why do you ask so many questions?" was repeated daily. At age seven, I asked my mother if she loved me, and she replied, "I wash your clothes and cook your food, don't I?"

And, yes, Mom did all that. She was an excellent cook and always had a clean house. And she made a birthday cake for my birthday every year with her favorite seven-minute frosting recipe.

"The child who is more intelligent, more sensitive, and more emotionally aware than other children can be so attuned to her parents' expectations that she does whatever it takes to fulfill these expectations while ignoring her feelings and needs. In becoming the "perfect" child of her parents' dreams, the gifted child loses something very precious. She loses her true self. In becoming her parents' ideal child, she locks away her true feelings in a kind of "glass cellar," the key to which is thrown away. The gifted child in this type of situation stops growing. Because he cannot develop and differentiate his true self, he feels empty, emotionally isolated, and "homeless." In adulthood, the child who has always tried to please his parents is constantly looking to others for approval." – Alice Miller, *The Drama of the Gifted Child*

Wow! That was me. I still question myself and look to others for approval and validation. The degree of that is much less, but it still exists!

My mother was raised in a Catholic home and was very poor. The Great Depression began when she was a young child. What an interesting name for that period in time. Her father was an alcoholic and stuttered. Her parents divorced during her ninth year, which was rare in 1932, especially for Catholics.

During the Great Depression (1929-1933), the number of children entering orphanages and institutions increased by fifty percent. Children suffered from malnutrition in addition to inadequate clothing. Even though families applied for government assistance and food, it was insufficient for survival. Fathers were emotionally distant, engaged in drinking alcohol, and deserted their families due to their inability to support them.

Grandpa's parents came to the United States from Holland on a boat and were quite wealthy. Grandpa inherited many acres of farmland. Grandpa lost the land, divorced Grandma, and was absent for many years with no one knowing his whereabouts. This scenario created abandonment issues for my mother, and her relationship with her father was troubled. Occasionally, my uncle would receive a phone call from a bar looking for a family member to remove Grandpa from the premises. Grandpa grew old and shared with me that he had regrets and wished that he would have made better choices. I know he loved Grandma and his family very much.

My Grandma was a kind and hard-working woman with the ability to show love. Grandma was a bootlegger for a time. People who illegally made, imported, or sold alcohol during Prohibition were called this term. Prohibition in the United States was a nationwide constitutional ban on the production, importation, transportation, and sale of alcoholic beverages from 1920 to 1933. She sold alcohol out of her home for money to feed her three children as jobs were scarce to none. I remember mom telling me that she hated it when men knocked on their door at one in the morning for a drink. Grandma later found employment cooking at a restaurant until retirement and passed soon after.

I vividly remember Grandma taking a picture of me when I was about eight years old. She bought me a pretty red floral dress with a matching hat and positioned me next to her blooming red rose trellis. I felt so special. I sensed that Grandma was the only one who loved me, although she never told me. But I could tell when she would invite me to spend a night with her and how she always smiled at me when I showed up at her door. She was the one person in my life that influenced my self-esteem. Grandma trusted me enough to varnish her cherished China cabinet at the age of ten. I was so proud until mom came to pick me up and said to Grandma, "You let *her,* do it? Look, she has it smeared all over the glass." My heart sank. Ironically, precisely fifty years later, I inherited that now antique piece of furniture and removed the varnish I had smudged on the glass with a sharp razor blade.

Mom repeated a story many times, sharing a painful childhood memory. One Christmas, she received a single gift of a spittoon for her habit of spitting. I could hear the hurt in her voice each time that story was told. She mentioned they were so poor that lard was spread on bread as butter was too expensive. As a child, she walked the railroad tracks with her two brothers looking for coal to burn at night to stay warm. Mom was blessed with the same sense of humor, tenacity, and strength as a woman that my grandma possessed. Her mother and her husband were two of the most influential people in her life that she depended on. She lost them both just three years apart, when in her late thirties. Left with three children, little money, and no life insurance, she sold dad's tools and truck before social security arrived for us children. She spent most of her time in her bedroom for more than a year before she finally sought help from a psychiatrist. After proper medication, she found employment remaining at that facility for twenty-three years until her retirement. Due to her ability to be frugal, she saved enough money to purchase a house for herself. Depression and anxiety crept in and out of her life, with her finally declaring that Paxil was her saving grace.

I don't remember my father much and have only a few memories I can count on one hand. He worked fifteen hours a day managing a gas station and repairing cars as a mechanic. He worked diligently to support his family and had few interactions with me, especially as the middle child. He was a stocky and handsome man, and it hurt much worse when he spanked. Thinking back, I wonder how it must have felt to come home after a long day at work and to have to spank your child at your spouse's request.

I recall mom's fear and anxiety each time she heard an ambulance siren, aware of dad's enlarged heart. The third heart attack took his life at the young age of forty-nine, just after my fifteenth birthday. I recall observing him sitting in a recliner in the evenings with his hand over his heart. There must have been a lot of concern and worry about his health and future for his family.

As he passed before I was born, I didn't know his father but was told he was a good man. But dad's mother was a strong, stern, and independent young widow with no nurturing skills. I remember observing the staves in her massive, laced corset bound firmly at the waist through her dress material. She wore thick, nylon nude-colored stockings with a heavy shine that were attached to garter belts. Grandma created a small business with a shop next to her house selling various art projects naming it Mamie's Gift Shop. I remember her washing clothes from water collected in a large rain barrel under a downspout. Her tiny house always smelled of Noxema and was kept warm with a single gas stove in her living room. In her eighties, she dug a root cellar for food storage with only a shovel.

My intention here is not to blame or come from a place of victimization, but to share my personal journey in my search for love. To understand this process, I must explain to you what I was missing. You don't usually miss what you don't have, but instincts told me something was just not right here. Many children grow up getting what they don't want or not getting what they need, and many are blessed to be born into a family with love expressed. I believe most people, including parents, do the best they can with the awareness, understanding, and knowledge they have at that time. Children model what they see. Children imitate and learn by watching and listening to others. The family they reside in is all they know, and they think this is normal.

Mary Trump shows us how emotional abuse is passed from generation to generation, although the Trump family considered their lives normal. Most of us never thought of how our childhood experiences shaped our behaviors. I recall viewing John Bradshaw's video on *The Family* with a friend. His response was," This explains my family. Why didn't anyone ever share this information with me before?" Again, "When the student is ready, the teacher appears."

When we arrive at a place of understanding ourselves and looking at our parents' and grandparents' parenting skills and beliefs, we can then make sense of why we did not get what we needed or got what we did not want and not pass judgment on anyone. We must let go of blaming our parents for how they influenced our lives in negative ways and take responsibility for ourselves. The hole you may be in may be the same hole your parents were trying to climb out of. No one is at fault. The only thing that matters is climbing out of that hole. Blame only takes away your power.

"The job of parents is to model. Modeling includes being a man or woman; how to relate intimately to another person; how to acknowledge and express emotions; how to fight fairly; how to have physical, emotional, and intellectual boundaries; how to communicate; how to cope and survive life's unending problems; how to be self-disciplined; and how to love oneself and another. Shame-based parents cannot do any of these. They simply don't know how. Being abandoned through the neglect of our developmental dependency needs is the major factor in

becoming an adult child. We grow up, and we look like adults. We walk and talk like adults, but beneath the surface is a little child who feels empty and needy, a child whose needs are insatiable because he has a child's needs in an adult body." - John Bradshaw

The family I knew dissipated in less than twenty-four hours. My brother left home on a Saturday evening. Dad suffered his third major heart attack and died the next morning. Mom regressed into a deep depression residing in her bedroom, and my sister, at the age of twelve, quit school roaming free. I remember crying uncontrollably when taps were played at my father's gravesite. My Uncle Jack moved toward me and placed his arms embracingly around my shoulders. It felt strange, as no one had ever given me physical comfort like that.

I assumed the responsibility and care for mom when she suffered from a nervous breakdown after dad's sudden death. She lost her beloved mother just three years prior. Most of her days were spent in her room crying or sleeping. Evenings included nightmares and screams from her bedroom. After getting her down the stairs, I heated a cup of coffee and lit a cigarette for her. Suddenly in conversation, she would lay her head on the table, raise it, and say, "What am I doing here?" This scenario continued for more than a year.

I recall a Friday night when there was a teen street dance downtown. I had a new dress and yearned to go. I asked the neighbor lady if she would stop over to visit mom so I could leave for an hour and not tell mom I had arranged it. I could not go and enjoy myself if I was worried about mom. Mom finally sought psychiatric help in a nearby city, received medication, and was advised to seek employment with the intent to focus on others. Mom found a job as a cook and remained there for twenty-three years until her retirement, slowly healing from her grief and shock.

My emotional growth was stunted at age fifteen, and that is also when I started to gain weight. I worked at a café a few days a week after school, and the food was free while working. I loved cherry cokes, fries, and broasted chicken and used food to cope. But what I was hungry for was attention, love, and affection. Unfortunately, emotional eating does not fix problems; it only makes them worse. It makes you feel shame and guilt by gaining weight. I did not understand that this was a coping skill at that time.

My one and only friend, Ann, moved in with us for a month after dad died. Her support and companionship helped us all cope and adjust. Ann and I remained friends for fifty-three years until her transition.

CHAPTER 3

♡

SEARCHING FOR
THE MISSING PIECE

"Hell, in my opinion, is never finding your
true self, never living your own life
or knowing who you are."
-   John Bradshaw

Most teenagers engage in sexual intercourse by the age of seventeen. The production of testosterone increases ten times in adolescent boys. The perfect partner is the young female with low self-esteem and self-concept who desires to be loved and touched. Everyone yearns for love as the flower yearns for the sun.

I loved caring for my doll as a child; bathing, dressing, and brushing her hair daily. Two months before Christmas, my mother took my only doll, Margaret, from me. When I opened my gift at Christmas, I finally understood why, as she was dressed in a new set of clothes with new hair that Grandma had tailored for her. I remember once a month mom would buy something special like a package of cookies. I had to wait for days until she was ready to open them.

My dream was to become a wife and stay-at-home mom caring for my children. I knew a child would love me unconditionally. I envisioned residing in a one-story house, complete with a garage, garden, flowers, and a white picket fence. My husband would be successfully employed and support our family financially.

I am pleased that getting pregnant out of wedlock or in high school does not carry the same shame it once did. In my teen years, the pregnant girl left town, delivered the baby, adopted it out, returning as if nothing had happened. Marrying the father was the other option.

The condition is pregnancy, but the blessing is the child. Everything happens for a reason, and the plan is perfect, but that is not understood until much later. Society can be cruel and judgmental to teen moms. Males do not have to bear the responsibility for the pregnancy. Guys are viewed as macho, patted on the back, and girls carry the judgment and shame of being a tramp. At least, that was the scenario in the sixties.

As a child, I was introverted and very naïve. Most who know me now cannot imagine this. Why did I always feel like I was different from everyone else and feel like I did not fit in? I must have appeared shy, weak, boring, and unconfident. Was it because I was asked each day, "What is wrong with you?" It is embarrassing to say now, but I did not think I looked like other females sexually.

A child's brain, until the age of seven, believes everything it hears. Neuroscience research suggests a child's brain functions precisely like a brain under hypnosis. Be mindful of what you say to children.

Possessing a highly sensitive and empathic nature, I knew I was different. I felt like wallpaper on a wall just observing others. Imagine a puzzle with a piece missing. That is how I felt inside. Some emotional neglect symptoms include feeling like something is missing, low self-esteem, being easily overwhelmed or discouraged, and having a pronounced sensitivity to rejection and perfectionism. That was me.

I knew it was going to be up to me to find the missing piece of my puzzle. I felt empty, sad, inadequate, and insecure. My spirit craved meaning, fulfillment, and connection. Change is available to us all. When we finally understand that no one will do it for us, we must go deep within ourselves and find the courage to move forward and seek change.

"A time comes in your life when you finally get it. When in the midst of all your fears and insanity, you stop dead in your tracks, and somewhere the voice inside your head cries out - ENOUGH!" – Sonny Carroll, *The Awakening*

Born a Taurus, my ruling planet is Venus, the hottest planet in our solar system. Ruling planets have the most influence over a zodiac sign. Venus is associated with love, human life, and relationships and is named after the ancient Roman goddess of love and beauty, called Aphrodite, in ancient Greece.

There is a saying, alternately attributed to Buddha Siddhartha Guatama Shakyamuni and the Theosophists, that goes.; "When the student is ready, the teacher will appear." Then I met Lisa.

Lisa was a new volunteer at the county food pantry I coordinated. During a break on our first day together, I shared with her the relationship I had with my deceased father and began crying. I soon opened up to her, trusting her immediately. I have never responded to anyone like this before, not even a counselor. When I started crying, she asked, "Are you OK?" I thought," No one had ever asked me that question before or acted as if they cared." It felt awkward to have someone ask me that. She took me under her wing, befriending and supporting me with her care and concern. It still brings tears to my eyes as I think of the deep soulful love I have for Lisa. She stated many times in our twenty-six-year relationship that she loves me beyond words. I imagine this is the same love that my heavenly guides and God have for me, too. I have since found that same love within myself for others.

I journeyed through eight years of reading hundreds of books on topics of child abuse and neglect, family dynamics, family dysfunction, addiction, mental illness, co-dependency, and the inner child within us all. I never had the desire to read and hated to read until there was a topic that interested me enough to want to educate myself on. And I did not become passionate about writing a book until I grew older and yearned to pass on the knowledge I acquired in this lifetime to future generations. Counseling with Lisa and professionals helped me gain greater insight, overcome obstacles, and strengthen my self-esteem. My earth angel, Lisa, supported me with unconditional love plus acceptance. She provided me with the tools I needed to endure the difficult steps of awareness, anger, grief, and finally, forgiveness and acceptance. Her supply of books was endless as I hungered for more knowledge.

I envision this as a type of gardening. First, you pull up those unwanted weeds, mix and prepare the soil with proper nutrients, plant healthy seeds, water, and nurture the new growth with sunlight and then enjoy the harvest.

Healing is a challenging and painful process requiring commitment and a lot of patience. Recovery is when individuals take charge of their lives, striving to reach their full potential. Support comes from relationships with people that are trustworthy as we learn, grow, and heal. Uncovering pain is comparable to removing the layers of an onion – the more you peel, the deeper you go into past wounds, but in those layers lies more understanding. When one aspect is healed, another will emerge. A variety of emotions are experienced, including denial, anger, confusion, depression, and sadness. Hiding under the emotion of anger is always sadness.

The experience can go from bad to worse before it gets better. We sometimes wonder if the pain will ever end. And there are periods when you have time to rest and reflect. But as each layer is removed, you gain more strength, insight, and healing, bringing you closer to your true self.

Acceptance and forgiveness happen after emotions are dealt with. New patterns of living with conscious awareness and moving toward mental, emotional, physical, and spiritual balance are necessary for preservation.

I asked Lisa many, many times, "Am I almost done?" She would reply," It's like peeling an onion and removing the layers. Your onion is getting smaller, sweetie."

Mom introduced me to John Bradshaw on the PBS *(Public Broadcasting Service)* series *Healing the Shame That Binds You* by taping the weekly programs and sending the videotapes home with me to watch. In this series, John Bradshaw reveals that shame is the driving force behind self-sabotaging behaviors. Shame is designed to halt behaviors but instead instills in a child negative thoughts and feelings about themselves. Shaming does not separate the action from the person. It affects the soul deeply, giving children a negative image of themselves and does little to correct behaviors. Shaming can destroy a person's life, creating addictions, anxiety, depression, compulsions, co-dependency, and can drive super achievers. It also limits our ability to be fully connected in relationships.

Bradshaw's many books have helped millions of people identify, understand, and address their shame. This information was the catalyst in my search for wholeness by understanding why I was the way I was. Why did I feel insecure, inadequate, and indifferent? The videos allowed me to understand my family dynamics. I realized that only *I* could amend the past and create personal happiness. Wow, that sounded like a massive task. I was expecting someone else to do it for me.

Bradshaw quoted a phrase from Gerard Manley Hopkins, a Jesuit priest and English poet, "What I do is me, for that I came." This statement struck deep within my soul. I wrote and taped this phrase to the refrigerator, and it remained there for a year. How powerful those words hit me as I was discovering my true self. I don't have to be like everyone else. It is OK to be me! And yes, I *am* different. And that is a good thing. I read all of John Bradshaw's books, and some twice. I traveled to St. Louis, Missouri, to see the author at a presentation of his new book, *The Family*. This man was my savior.

"Family secrets can go back for generations. They can be about suicides, homicides, incest, abortions, addictions, public loss of face, financial disaster, etc. All the secrets get acted out. This is the power of toxic shame." - John Bradshaw

One day my sister noticed a book lying on my table entitled *The Family*. She picked it up, read the front cover, and said, "There's nothing wrong with our family," and set it firmly down. You don't know what you don't know, and most of us think that all families are as ours was. Many families have an unwritten but very firm and understood rule that it is not allowed to talk about certain things.

I recall the first time I saw a man in a bar passing around his wife and kids' photos. I was amazed that a father would do this. I also remember how reluctant I was to visit my aunt. She greeted each one of us with a hug, and I couldn't wait until it was over. It felt strange, embarrassing, and uncomfortable. Today, this is me! I enjoy greeting others when they arrive with a hug and with another hug and an "I love you" when they leave. When in my twenties, I watched the soap opera *Days of Our Lives*. When viewing two lovers looking lovingly into each other's eyes, I wondered if there were couples who did experience that in their relationships. I would think, "I want that."

Inner child work can be accomplished by yourself or with a therapist. Working with Lisa was beneficial, but I needed additional validation from counselors. Dr. Marty was my first and favorite counselor/psychologist. He was the first man I encountered in my life who was kind and caring. His voice was gentle, looking me in the eyes as he listened, but I did not always look at him. I was full of shame and embarrassment.

I have since learned that an Emotional Freedom Technique (EFT) practitioner can tap out undesired emotions and pain, accelerating the healing process compared to talk therapy. Counseling and talk therapy can take months or years to achieve results, but with EFT, there are more rapid outcomes.

In Zen Master Thich Nhat Hanh's book, *Reconciliation,* this wise Buddhist states that, "Inside each one of us is a young suffering child and we try to forget the pain." Most often, when we feel pain from a place deep within us, it is our inner child. Attempting to forget the pain or pushing it down deeper results in more pain. Most of us have encountered some woundedness tied to our inner child. Perhaps there was abuse, a broken family, or our best friend moved away. When we begin to understand that some of our fears and phobias as adults are tied to our inner child, then transformation can occur.

The only way out is through. You can keep trying to escape reality by gambling, drinking, drugs, cheating, promiscuity, eating a bag of chips, watching TV all day, or sleeping. But sooner or later, it will catch up with you as another divorce, illness, accident, emotional meltdown, a pile of debt, or as a patient of Dr. Now on the television series *My 600 lb. Life.*

Concerning obesity, bypassing the pain with a "bypass" will erase the physical aspects but not the core issues. Individuals can switch addictions if core issues are not addressed and healed. I've met individuals who stop drinking alcohol and develop a sugar addiction. Another person I met stopped using cocaine and became a minister. A few years later, his wife divorced him due to obsessing over his parish and neglecting his family. Other examples may include substituting food for shopping, gambling for pornography, smoking for eating, and the list goes on.

"Addiction is a special kind of hell. It takes the soul of the addict and breaks the hearts of those who love them." So many loved ones departed from my life because of addiction. Cigarettes, drugs, alcohol, and codependency have taken their lives. We all will die of something, but watching someone near and dear to you suffer is extremely heartbreaking.

One man I knew entered into treatment for a gambling addiction and switched addictions every month. In the first month of treatment, he could not consume enough raisin bran cereal. The following month he purchased thirty-four new shirts, and in the third month, he could stop viewing pornography. Finding relief from problems by turning to a substance or excessive behaviors risks the development of an addiction. Problems do not go away until they are addressed, healed, and solved. This person continued substituting addictions until core issues were healed.

"The key to treating addiction replacement is addressing the underlying cause of compulsive behavior, thoughts, and actions through therapy. The only way to fully put a stop to replacement addictions is

by addressing any unconscious emotion and working through them." - Jeffrey Juergens

In my forties, I undertook inner child work for the first time on Bradshaw's PBS series. Finding your vulnerable and sensitive inner child requires meditation with a clear mind with no expectations. I reclaimed little Mary Marcia at age five on the school playground I attended as a child. She was wearing a plaid dress and running around a merry-go-round. The book suggested finding a photo of yourself at this young age and placing it where you could look at it every day as an attempt to bond. It is easier to love a child than it is to love your adult self. I was instructed to tell Mary Marcia that I loved her, understood her pain, and was there to parent her now with the love, understanding, and respect she deserves. It felt awkward talking to her. At first, there was no connection.

The following year I purchased Bradshaw's book *Homecoming: Reclaiming and Championing Your Inner Child,* and I committed to this work again. It was much more detailed and included numerous written assignments such as writing your life story and including hurtful incidents. It was impressive how the pen kept flowing. Letters to parents, teachers, friends, or other family members who have mistreated you are written with the non-dominant hand. Doing this integrates the right and left-brain hemispheres. This technique is also powerful as the script resembles a child's writing. Conversations with your inner child can be written using your dominant hand (adult self) corresponding to the child, and the child responds with the non-dominant hand.

I rescued my child once again at age fifteen; Mary Marcia was sitting at a bay window watching cars drive by. After finding Mary Marcia at this age, I parted my hair on the side, bought some pink lipstick, and wanted to go dancing again. I wore peppermint pink lipstick in my teens. When out on the town dancing and drinking alcohol, friends noticed my voice pitch would change, and I exhibited unfamiliar behavior. That was Mary Marcia. A friend kept insisting I had *MPD* (Multiple Personality Disorder), so I set up an appointment with a professional in that field. It was a relief to learn I was reuniting with Mary Marcia at age fifteen as I disconnected from her emotionally when my father passed. My family noticed my behaviors were changing. Mom was calling it a mid-life crisis. It was challenging for family members to observe my new and strange behaviors. But that is when the fun and the difficult lessons began! I picked up where I left off so many years ago. My children were grown, and I was about to experience my late teens at age forty-six.

I don't believe the healing process is ever 100% finished, but the most challenging part of that tunnel of change lasted eight years. It wasn't until then that I felt the sunshine on my face. Forgiveness took the longest. As much as I wanted it to transpire, it could not be forced.

Avoiding conflict is a clear sign of fearing anger. Conflict is a natural part of life. We often neglect to assert ourselves, including our feelings and opinions, because we have learned that anger should be avoided. In accepting that anger is an emotion like any other, new skills can be developed to release it.

Anger is a natural, healthy emotion that everyone experiences. Feeling anger by cursing, sarcasm, yelling, arguing, hitting a wall, or throwing things on the floor is normal and a basic human emotion. But when it confuses your judgment, there may be repressed emotions such as sadness, being overwhelmed, loneliness, guilt, contempt, shame, fear, frustration, insecurity, or embarrassment. Anger might be expressed when someone feels rejected or threatened, has experienced an emotional or physical situation, or has some sort of loss. The surroundings and conditions in which one lives, in particular abuse, stress, financial issues, or being immersed with obligations, will also trigger and inflate anger. Anger can harm us physically as well as mentally.

There are many myths about anger. Nice people do not feel anger. If we get angry with someone, they will go away, which means we do not love them. If someone gets angry with us, they don't love us anymore. We were told that anger is a sin. Many of us have swallowed our anger shoving it down into our stomachs, biting our tongues, let it jump around in our heads, creating a headache and making us nervous. If you were regularly scolded, lectured, or punished, your anger had to be subdued. We medicate it, give it a cookie or a drink, and get depressed.

Children who grew up in a significantly dysfunctional household and did not get their physical, emotional, and psychological needs met by their parents store this accumulated anger inside. Unconscious on your part, this emotion can be triggered by anything in your life that reawakens it. Releasing anger inappropriately can harm your relationships, raise your blood pressure, damage your health, and even shorten your life. Research shows a higher risk of having a heart attack within two hours after an anger outburst, chest pain, stroke, and irregular heart rhythms.

When allowing ourselves to feel anger, we become more alive. We can now grieve what's been long-held tight in our hearts. After anger is released, followed by the cleansing waters of sadness, it creates a space to allow joy and inner peace to come through. Allowing your pent-up anger to be released in a safe and controlled environment is an excellent way to let it go and make peace with it.

Have you ever acted impulsively, in the heat of the moment, and said something you didn't mean to say? I did. After you gave in to your anger and lost control, you reviewed the situation blamelessly and ended up hurting loved ones over something irrelevant. Even with an apology, the penance you suffer for the act seems like it takes forever.

Negative emotions can accumulate, and anger can rear its ugly head with minor issues. My ex-husband became furious with rage if he saw any water on the kitchen counter. I walked on eggshells for many years, trying to keep the children quiet and composed and covering for his anger so their feelings were not hurt. That emotional heaviness caused chronic sinus headaches and constipation in me for decades. People who are triggered easily usually have past unresolved issues.

The EFT procedure is clinically proven to reduce surface and deep-seated anger, anxiety, tension, stress, depression, and the emotions associated with past adverse events. With this release, happiness, health and vitality are restored. EFT can take you to those experiences buried deep down within you and release the triggers and root causes of anger.

Lisa and I began to collect glass jars in preparation for anger work. She knew the day would come, and it did. I don't remember what in particular I was upset about, but she loaded the boxes of glass in the car and said, "Let's go."

Lisa drove us to an old dump site outside the city limits. She said, "OK. Get angry and start throwing." I reluctantly tossed a jar at a cement culvert but felt nothing. Encouraging the release of the monster, she asked, "What about this person, and what happened?" "What about this incident, etc." I began feeling rage, throwing harder and faster.

Then the anger monster appeared, making beastly and dreadful sounds. I felt this pure rage coming from deep within me. When allowing the feelings of anger, sadness, and joy, we can heal, becoming more alive. When the sleeping anger monster is freed from its cage and finally gets to roar, we allow ourselves to grieve what's been long-held tight in our chest. And when this anger is felt and released, followed by the cleansing waters of sadness and tears, the void can be filled with joy, love, and forgiveness, and our spirit is renewed. Lisa drove me back to my lonely apartment, and I slept for the rest of the afternoon. How therapeutic this event was in moving forward!

The lyrics from the song *Because You Loved Me* declare all the emotions I have for my angel, Lisa. No one had ever displayed that degree of love to me before I met her. Earth angels are evolved spiritual beings appearing in human form on our planet to serve humanity. They have a calling at the soul level to help others, spread kindness, compassion, and bring love and light to the world. Imperfect like all of humanity, they make mistakes, have challenges, and feel disconnected at times.

Every one of us is born with an ego connecting us to the external world. The ego allows us to forget who we were in spirit form. It is as necessary as is the mind and intellect. Ego gives us insight, guiding our behavior in both positive and negative ways. The English word ego is the Latin word for *I*. Some say that your ego is your false self, the negative side of us, and it needs to be diffused. Your ego is your personality, conscious mind, identity, self-image, and social mask. It is how you see yourself. The ego creates labels, roles, and stories of who we think we are. It wants to control and is sustained with power. In accepting our ego, we acknowledge our human self. Without it, creativity and drive are lost.

The driving force of the ego is fear. Anger, greed, lust, and discrimination are all based on fear. The ego will help you play the victim role. The negative side of the ego is defined as "Edging God Out."

The ego can manifest as self-esteem, self-direction, moral development, vanity, pride, judgment, arrogance, and prejudice. In exaggerated cases, the ego can be insidious, tempting us with the need to control, the lust for power, and the obsession for material things. I have observed this in CEOs, politicians, physicians, and ministers. No one is exempt. The ego knows our weaknesses, secret desires, inhibitions, and denials, and will use them against us, disconnecting us from the Divine.

Managing the ego is necessary for peace of mind. Live consciously and be aware of your choices and why you are making them. The old Arab proverb states it perfectly. "The words of the tongue should have three gatekeepers. Before words get past the lips, the first gatekeeper asks, "Is it true?" The second gatekeeper asks," Is it kind?" and the third gatekeeper asks," Is it necessary?"

All of us judge. The root of all judgment comes from our egos. When viewing someone behaving in a way that we disagree with, we think, "I would never act like that! I would never do that. At least I work." Putting someone else down makes us feel better about ourselves. The work of our ego distracts us from our shortcomings. It is essential to remind ourselves that everyone's experience is unique. How can we predict how we would react if we had to walk in their shoes? Everyone has fears, doubts, and baggage that we cannot see. When we judge, we are only looking at the part of someone visible to us. With the ability to know what was going on inside them, their actions and behaviors might have made more sense.

"It is nearly impossible to hate anyone whose story you know," states writer Andrew Solomon. There are always opportunities to learn and grow in the sense of understanding another. When we judge, we focus on someone's negative qualities and disregard their good ones. Sometimes, it is a reflection of something we refuse to see in ourselves. Rev. Sky St. John used to remind us, "If you spot it, you got it." When you understand and love your ego, fear is removed, and it will threaten you less. Teach it humility through compassion and serving others.

People used to ask me if I was on *Facebook*. I had no interest in sharing my life with others or posting photos. I felt it was a way for others to brag about themselves. When *My Journey Finding Love* was published, Amazon encouraged me to join *Facebook* to advertise and promote my book. I connected with people I had no contact with for over thirty years. I found this awesome and realized it was a new pathway to communicate without spending hours on the phone. Like texting, I loved the ability to reply to others at a convenient time. I liked that! But I was astonished at the excessiveness of the selfies that some were posting. I also recognized that several individuals would post ten to twelve times a day. I was curious as to the psychological need for such self-indulgence and began to research this. Psychology and the study of people and their behaviors have always interested me. When younger, my children and husband would call me Marlena, referring to the psychiatrist Dr. Marlena Evans on *Days of Our Lives.*

I discovered that in 2014 the term *selfitis* was labeled as a mental condition that makes someone feel compelled to take selfies and post them for others to see, such as on their social media accounts. A study done by *Nottingham Trent University* developed a scale of borderline, acute, or chronic as to how serious *selfitis* can be. The study also revealed that those with the disorder had a need to increase their self-esteem to improve their mood, sought attention, had a desire to connect with their environment, and were socially competitive. A 2015 study in the issue of *Personality and Individual Differences* looked at traits including narcissism, psychopathy, manipulation, and self-objection. A person's mental health played a vital role in how many photos of oneself were posted and how much retouching of the images was performed. Those who were labeled narcissistic displayed psychopathic tendencies and those who viewed their bodies as objects based on self-worth posted the most selfies. The study concluded that this group did not fall into a healthy self-confidence region with good mental health.

Observe and analyze your ego. Be honest with what you see. You cannot attempt to change what you do not acknowledge about yourself. We can balance our ego by giving up the need to be correct, listen, and encourage others by giving our support, love, and attention. Also, we can try to understand the human ego, and practice forgiveness and let go. By embracing and honoring our ego, it can be seen as a valid part of ourselves. Know that it is an essential part of our human condition and take responsibility for it.

Self-justification is like quicksand and can draw us deeper into destruction. It blocks our ability to recognize our errors and correct them. It distorts our reality keeping us misinformed and the ability to examine issues clearly and effectively. It prolongs arguments and destroys relationships between lovers, families, friends, and nations. It keeps us from letting go of unhealthy habits and permits the guilty to avoid taking responsibility for their actions. Many professionals refuse to change outdated attitudes and procedures that can harm the public due to self-justification and self-righteousness.

Apologizing is the greatest gift we can give to ourselves and to someone we hurt. When we take responsibility for our words and actions respect is earned. Most of us find it welcoming and open-hearted when people admit to their wrongdoing. We yearn to hear politicians, leaders, and our relatives say, "Yes, I screwed up. I apologize, and now I want to fix it." Hearing this frees us and allows us to do the same.

"Apologies aren't meant to change the past, they are meant to change the future." - Kevin Hancock

The opposite of forgiveness is resentment and revenge keeping you in pain. Spending your time in a negative memory will only cause you more suffering and let the past and others control you. There is always have a choice as to how to react to something. I discovered that forgiveness is a gift that you give to yourself. The pain that you feel is not hurting them. It is hurting you. Fighting evil with evil does not help anyone. It's not about agreeing that what they did was OK. It's about you refusing to punish yourself any longer because of what happened. Attempt to realize the other person's woundedness, let it go, and forgive their soul. Forgiveness and letting go are the same. Look for and learn the lessons from that experience. Forgiveness is a process. But when you do not forgive, you give away your power. Can you imagine a world where everyone would forgive and let go of the past?

"The weak can never forgive. Forgiveness is the attribute of the strong. An eye for an eye only ends up making the whole world blind." - Mahatma Gandhi

The mind is the gatekeeper for your heart and soul. No one reserves the right to abuse you, not even your family. If you were born into a family devoid of love and tenderness, you are not obligated to keep them in your life. You don't have to accept toxic people because they are family. Toxic people will hold you back. They will never deserve you. If someone continues to cause you disharmony, keep them at a distance. We don't have to keep ourselves open to abuse and disrespect. That is self-care.

Forgiving yourself is more complicated than forgiving others, but just as important. Know that you deserve forgiveness. Each one of us is human and prone to making mistakes. Expecting perfection in others or yourself only creates unnecessary conflict and negativity within you. Forgiving yourself for the mistakes you've made can release you from self-misery, hate, and regret.

Accept your humanness. The emotions within your being are capable of affecting your physical and mental health. Negative emotions can cause depression, cardiovascular problems, and affect immune function.

Ask yourself, "What can I do to be forgiven?" The simple phrase, "I am sorry" is short but profoundly powerful. But say it sincerely while looking into the other person's eyes. Sometimes writing a letter is easier. Accept the fact that you caused someone hurt, grief, and pain. Completely own the part you played in the interaction and make amends. Replace the word *mistake* with the *lesson* and learn from it. Receiving forgiveness alleviates guilt and shame. EFT is very effective in clearing these emotions and beliefs attached to them.

"Inner peace can be reached only when we practice forgiveness. Forgiveness is letting go of the past and is, therefore, the means for correcting our misperceptions." - Gerald Jampolsky

Sometimes I recall a situation I used to endure and think, "I can't believe that was me!" Now, I would never allow someone to call me *stupid* or continue a hopeless relationship with an alcoholic or addict. That is genuine proof that you have grown. When you surrender and let go of the past, only then can you be fully alive and live in the present moment.

The present is a gift. I believe most of us do the best we can with the knowledge, wisdom, understanding, and awareness we have at that time in our lives. Remember, our mission here is to grow and learn in this earth school called life.

"When you change the way you look at things, the things you look at change." - Wayne Dyer ✗

In later years, when mom asked me," What is wrong with you?" I confidently replied," Mother, there is nothing wrong with me. There is everything right with me." My mother was in my life for a major purpose and cause. I love and miss her with all of my heart and love her beyond words. The insight and feelings we discovered together brought us both a love and a relationship I had always desired. I appreciated the opportunity to share my admiration and love with her before she transitioned eleven years ago. I talk to her daily and still dream of her many times a week. I feel her when we are together in the dream state, which helps me deal with her earthly loss.

With tears in my eyes as I write this, I miss her deeply. I have the utmost respect and honor for this unique and special woman whose strength, tenacity, strong faith, belief in the power of prayer, trust in God, redeeming humor, and endurance sustained her through a difficult life. Even while suffering from lung cancer for eighteen months, she always declared, "There is always someone somewhere who has it worse."

I understand why my parents could not give me what I needed as a child by putting myself in their circumstances. With that understanding came forgiveness with a love that mom and I shared, exceeding measures and limitations. We discussed and agreed that whoever left this earth first would be there to assist the other with their entrance into the next dimension. I know she will be there to greet me with open arms and have the Scrabble board ready.

A few months after mom's soul left this dimension, I posed a series of questions to my pendulum. Pendulum divination is one of the oldest methods for receiving information from your higher guides, guardian angels, and spiritual teachers.

Dowsing is a form of divination locating groundwater, buried metals, gemstones, oil, gravesites, and many other objects and materials without scientific equipment.

A pendulum is a weighted object suspended from a string or chain so that it can swing freely. You ask the questions. Acting as a receiver or transmitter, you will receive a *yes* or *no* answer depending on the swing. In my case, it also has a sense of humor, giving me a *duh*. Mastering it reminds me of learning how to ride a bike. Once learned, it's not forgotten.

I remember as a child using a sewing needle suspended from a thread, placing it over a wrist. Horizontal and vertical swings indicate a boy or girl child in the future. The longer the swing was still, indicate the length of time between pregnancies. When the number of children was complete, the needle would stop. For me, the details I received back then were correct.

I received information from my pendulum that mom would reincarnate in eighteen months into this family as a female. Eighteen months later, my granddaughter gave birth to a baby girl. How excited I was the day she was born! Mom said she might return a politician. Time will tell.

Reincarnation occurs when the soul returns to the physical realm in a new body. Buddhism states the soul will usually reincarnate generally between forty-nine days and two years after death. In Christianity, the belief is that reincarnation can occur any time after death.

Have you heard of someone who is called an old soul? Old souls tend to have a greater sense of knowledge and wisdom. They can feel out of place and not relate well to others their age and have a wealth of unexplained inner wisdom. Many have a sense that they have been here before. Information received by a psychic revealed I lived in three hundred and forty-five incarnations. I suspect I must be a slow learner.

Dr. Ian Stevenson, former professor of psychiatry at the *University of Virginia School of Medicine,* former chair of the Department of Psychiatry and Neurology, dedicated most of his career to finding evidence of reincarnation until he died in 2007. Dr. Stevenson claims to have found over three thousand examples of reincarnation during this time, which he shared with the scientific community.

Dr. Stevenson is one of many scientists to have evidence of reincarnation. Dr. Jim B. Tucker, a child psychologist and professor of *Psychiatry and Neurobehavioral Sciences* at the University of Virginia School of Medicine, researched children for over four decades who claim to remember previous lives, including natal and prenatal memories. Dr. Tucker took over the research of Dr. Stevenson upon his retirement in 2001.

Many declare that we establish a Pre-Birth Plan with a council of elders with our guides and can choose everything in our next lifetime, including our parents and the location where we will be born. Goals, challenges, roles, and experiences are selected. After the plan is in place, we are born and forget the plan and who we are. Forgetting is an essential part of the cycle. It's how to really get to know ourselves and fully live the current life we are living. The Pre-Birth Plan is set in place, but free will gives us the ability to create any reality we choose to live in. If certain situations are meant to be experienced, some things are out of our control.

I believe everyone is in our lives for a reason. I firmly believe in reincarnation. It just makes sense. I visualize two souls discussing and planning their next lifetime together with assistance from angel guides. "I will be your mother in your next life, allowing you the opportunity to discover more about love. With this plan, we both will evolve." Now talk about the perfect plan!

There are no accidents in life. There is synchronicity. Everything happens for a reason. The people in our lives show up when needed. All of humanity is linked together as part of the Universe. Unconscious vibes are sent out into the universe, attracting the people, events, and opportunities necessary when we are ready. It is not by chance that I met Lisa and others who were highly instrumental in my life lessons and inspirations.

When you wish to co-create with God, it is essential to believe it can happen and then let it go. Don't worry about the how's or why's. However, it may not precisely appear as you would expect. Trust the process, believing that everything happens for your highest good.

In the book *In God's Truth* by Nick Bunick, the author states there are four different elements that we are born with or are exposed to that influence who we are in this lifetime.

The first element is our genes inherited from our biological parents. The second element is the environment in which we grow up. The third is the astral plane, the position of the planets in the heavenly bodies at the time of our birth. And the fourth element that influences your present life is your experiences in past lives.

This explains why four children born of the same family, who inherit the same genes and were raised in precisely the same environment, can be different. These souls bring with them the talents and skills that have been developed in other lifetimes. Karmic rewards and debt are also paid for or collected.

The relationship between cause and effect is not limited to the physical. Karma reflects the Third Law of Motion. "For every action, there is an equal and opposite reaction." Good deeds are rewarded, and evil deeds have consequences. The behavioral guide to karma is based on the *Golden Rule*. There is a balance of energy that serves as a teaching of responsibility for all of us. "We reap what we sow."

Sadly, I discovered that our man-made justice system can be manipulated by people who use weaknesses and loopholes to their advantage. Many of you would be shocked to discover how easily the court system can be manipulated by the affluent and powerful. But karma cannot be escaped by anyone. The cycle of karma progresses to the highest level of existence until we all become one with the Universe.

CHAPTER 4

♡

HEALTHY LOVE, NURTURING RELATIONSHIPS

"Insanity is doing the same thing, over and over again, but expecting different results."
- Albert Einstein

C hildren who grow up without love and affection are unable to experience happiness and a sense of belonging. They feel alone in the world and cannot develop intimacy in relationships and continue to look for the prince/princess who will sweep them off their feet. The word *attachment* is defined as a heartfelt bond between two people where there is closeness and security. Attachment theory explains how the parent and child relationship influences the ability to regulate negative emotions, thrive in a relationship, and manage disagreements. Unconsciously, love is learned by the love we are shown in our family of origin.

Everyone walks out of their childhood with a story to tell. It could include traditions such as driving to Grandma's in Iowa every year on Thanksgiving; attending church services on Christmas Eve, or taking a family vacation to a lake every summer. Then there are the memories we would like to forget, like when our father came home drunk and punched a hole in the wall, the time the correctional officers came and took our brother to prison, when our parents divorced, or how we cried when saying goodbye to friends before moving to another state.

Love addicts seek someone to make them feel whole. They continually search for the perfect one. Craving the rush of a new love feeling, they quit when the high fades, not giving the relationship a chance to mature into something deeper and more meaningful. It is reasonable to want to spend a lot of time with your new love in the beginning. There is a chemical reaction in your brain that causes the production of dopamine during the honeymoon period. It is very similar to the feeling of using cocaine. In time, you get your head out of the clouds and start seeing reality. His quirks begin to annoy you. He repeats himself a lot and leaves the toilet seat up. It doesn't always mean you're any less in love with your partner. Young love grows into mature love. Security and friendship evoke deeper meaning to the union.

"Love at first sight is your hormones playing tricks on you. Falling in love, I say, is a chemical cocktail of D.O.S.E. (dopamine, oxytocin, serotonin, and endorphins) - the hormones that control our pleasure, love, happiness, and well-being receptors. When you fall in love at first sight, you are falling more in lust. The hormones secreted at that first initial interaction are dopamine (pleasure), testosterone, and estrogen - both sex hormones." - Dr. Tara Swart

Remember, puppy love? The first time someone held your hand, and you felt a sensation never felt?

Wow, you think this must be love! Everyone has a particular definition of love, and we love in different ways. Love is the highest form of energy in our consciousness, and this emotion can influence behavior. The potential and need to be loved are born in all of us.

Sometimes the love shown in our family of origin is not a healthy and nurturing type of love. But what we learned about love in childhood can be unlearned, but it takes time. The first step is to recognize that we did not get the needed love we wanted and realize its effects.

Learning how to love is determined by how you grow up, the people in your life, and your experiences. Children make unconscious observations on how relationships work by watching their parents. With parents as our first teachers, they are not always the best models. Children think their parents are perfect without knowing and understanding that parents are human beings here to learn as we are. When this is discovered, the child is disappointed and confused, realizing their sense of dependency has decreased.

Believing in fairy tales, I was expecting to meet my knight in shining armor, and he would make me happy. Happily, ever-after does not exist. Neither does Prince Charming. Living life as a wife and mother was all I needed or wanted. Fairy tales are misleading for little girls.

"Little girls are taught fairy tales that are filled with magic. Cinderella is taught to wait in the kitchen for a guy with the right shoe! Snow White is given the message that if she waits long enough, her prince will come. On a literal level, that story tells women that

their destiny depends on waiting for a necrophile (someone who likes to kiss dead people) to stumble through the woods at the right time. Not a pretty picture!" - John Bradshaw, *Homecoming: Reclaiming and Healing Your Inner Child.*

When you *need* someone to be happy in life, this is not love; it is codependency. Codependents make the best nurses, doctors, EMTs, etc. However, when you give more to others, neglecting your own needs or at your own expense, this can become an addiction. As the second child in the family order, I desperately wanted to please my parents in everything I did. I believe this was a contributor for me as well.

I recall a counselor asking me, "What do you like to do for fun?" I pondered the question and stumbled when replying, "Go on picnics." I hardly ever went on picnics! I had no sense of who I was. That led to many questions about fostering self-discovery. I asked myself, "What is my purpose here? Who am I? What do I like to do? What do I want to do?" I had no idea!

Codependency and enmeshment are similar, but not the same. In an enmeshed relationship, one is usually narcissistic, and the other is codependent. A good indication of an enmeshed relationship is when your happiness, contentment, and self-esteem rely on this relationship. Without the ability to talk to this person or be with them, a feeling of loneliness will increase to the point of irrational desires to reconnect. Focusing your attention on building a healthy relationship with yourself is the first step to psychological health.

There is no better way to discover yourself than in a relationship with someone. Honest communication can solve ninety percent of most problems. Everyone's needs are different, and those needs are to be communicated if we want others to give us what we desire. It is harder to repair or create a healthy relationship when partners play the blame game. Sharing feelings is more important than being right or wrong. It is necessary to show genuine care about each other's feelings and emotions.

Boundary setting is a skill and should be set in a relationship as soon as possible. Letting the other person know what you want and need is as important as what you will not tolerate in the relationship. But we don't usually think about this until manipulation, alienation, and abuse occur. You cannot assume your partner has the same feelings as you. Boundaries create mutual understanding and respect.

"Relationships are where we take our recovery show on the road." - Melody Beattie, *The Language of Letting Go*

Every relationship is unique. One person may make more money, have more time to pick up groceries, enjoy paying the bills, make supper, etc. If both are OK with these duties and it works, who cares what others think? There is always a give and take. There will always be differences in points of view and values. People grow, and change, and lessons never stop.

The best thing in the world is to love and be loved. To love who you are and love what you do. To never know love and not discover your true self is living a life without meaning.

"I used to spend so much time reacting and responding to everyone else that my life had no direction. Other people's lives, problems, and wants set the course for my life. Once I realized it was okay for me to think about and identify what I wanted, remarkable things began to take place in my life."- Melody Beattie, *The Language of Letting Go*

Our impulse to be kind and responsive to others is both humanistic and spiritual. Care and compassion feel rewarding and nurturing. Love is seeing what others need and, if possible, giving it to them. Giving of ourselves without neglecting our own needs and wants is a healthy balance of compassion. But know that you can never please a person who is not happy with themselves. It can be painfully difficult to have a relationship with a person who has a mental illness. Personal relationships with bipolar individuals have taught me to expect the unexpected. If the connection is exhausting or toxic to you, the decision to end it may be in your best interest.

Sacrifice will not make you a saint, nor will it bring you wholeness and fulfillment. When codependents die, they see someone else's life flash before them. That could have been me! A line from Hamlet, written by William Shakespeare states: "This above all things: to thine own self be true" (3.1.81).

If I could keep only five of the many books in my library, one of them would be *The Language of Letting Go* by Melody Beattie. These daily meditations for codependents have been my bible for over twenty years. I especially appreciate the back index allowing you to look for the issue, problem or concern, and read the advice, affirmation, and prayer. I gifted this book to each of my children and a niece.

Self-care is difficult for co-dependents focusing on other people's needs, problems, and feelings rather than taking care of themselves. Some grow up without role models to demonstrate and validate that their feelings are legitimate and necessary, feeling unworthy of love. In the fifties and sixties, parochial schools taught that selflessness was noble and a form of sacrifice for sin. Modeling the lives of the poor saints neglecting personal needs, and caring only for others taught us that this would bring us closer to God's reward. Know that your feelings are as valid as anyone else's. You are worthy, and you are important. Pay attention to your needs and wants, embracing the image and likeness of God that you are.

After all, in the end, it will be just you and God. All relationships end whether someone leaves you, you leave them, or in death. Everyone who comes into your life is there for a reason—even the person who passes you with a smile to brighten your day. If you ask for guidance and support, the Universe will provide someone who will show up to help. If it is time for a lesson to learn and grow, a teacher will appear. These relationships can end suddenly when a task or lesson is learned.

Relationships ending can teach you to rely only on yourself. As people come and go into our lives, we learn that we are the captain of our ship, know what is best for us, and can co-create with God a new chapter in our lives. It is normal to go through the grieving process when a relationship ends, but don't let the sadness cripple you. Pick yourself up, dust yourself off, and move forward.

Change is inevitable. Change is an unavoidable part of life as nothing lasts forever. When staying open and surrendering, growth is possible in this lifetime, and we courageously flow with change, adapting accordingly. Neuroscience tells us that it is possible to transform and deliberately rewire our brains. An emotion lasts only ninety seconds from the moment it's triggered, and a habit takes twenty-one days to form. With this incredible adaptability, we can flow with times of change again and again.

There are two choices when we hit rock bottom. We can just give up, throw in the towel or say, "Enough is enough." Facing up to challenges in life gives us strength and later puts us in a position to help others. Grit your teeth and force a smile, thanking the Universe for the opportunity to learn what you need. I love the song, " I get knocked down, but I get up again, you are never gonna keep me down," by Chumbawamba.

"Everyone says love hurts, but that is not true. Loneliness hurts. Rejection hurts. Losing someone hurts. Envy hurts. Everyone gets these things confused with love, but in reality, love is the only thing in this world that covers up all pain and makes someone feel wonderful again. Love is the only thing in this world that does not hurt." - Mesa Selimovic

Dysfunctional families are primarily the result of two adults, one abusive and the other codependent.

Untreated mental illness and addictions (such as substance abuse, including alcohol) can also be components.

Codependents have a false sense of security and happiness and will seek a partner to take care of. Needy individuals with low self-esteem will seek a partner who will take care of them. At the age of eighteen, my mother married my father, who was nine years older than her. Her father was absent for half of her childhood.

Codependents feel valued only when they please others. Possessing very low self-esteem, they find it difficult to know what they want and need. When parents don't know how to help you feel special and lovable, you develop a distorted view of yourself as unimportant and unlovable. You may have been ignored, shamed, or yelled at when you asked for something. Now, you give too much and try to fix others. When your partner is not giving back and just takes, your relationship will not prosper. I have encountered many takers in this world, and they are not that hard to find when you are a giver. You may keep hoping that your partner will change, but you get more depressed and angrier when they don't. The classic model is the codependent and the alcoholic. It's a toxic mix of two unhealthy adults attempting to create a happy and fulfilling relationship. This was my first husband and me.

Recently I heard the term *trauma bonding*. It usually occurs when a narcissist is repeatedly abusive to another person. The narcissist requires validation and love from the person being abused. This can happen in romantic relationships, with colleagues, family members, and friends. The narcissist will shower you with flattery, love, and appreciation to gain your affection. After winning your trust, they make you heavily depend on them for love and validation. Gradually they will criticize, blame you, and become more demanding. They will never be wrong. You will doubt your own perceptions and believe everything is your fault, so you give in and lose *yourself*. Fighting back only makes things worse and you get addicted to the highs and lows.

This type of relationship will have hostile communication, a lack of trust, controlling behaviors, frequent lying, and you will do all the giving feeling drained.

Leaving a toxic relationship is not easy and takes lots of courage and help from friends, family, and professionals. You have to commit to change, surround yourself with positivity, and stick with it. The person will try to control you and want you to fight back and your feelings will bounce around like a ball. You will go through the stages of grief as the relationship is dead. Those of us who have experienced this know how difficult it will be, but the rewards will be tremendous.

A healthy relationship is composed of mutual trust, excellent communication, patience, empathy, appreciation, respect, and love. When two people come together in a relationship, many adjustments have to be made. I agree that the timeline to build a good solid foundation is five years. Love is the glue that keeps the connection stable and strong, as well as commitment from both individuals.

"In our differences, we grow, in our sameness, we connect." - Virginia Satir

Healthy love is accepting someone without wanting to change them. We cannot change anyone. We can only change ourselves and how we react to them. It is mandatory to respect the other person's freedom. Couples who enjoy their independence, sharing experiences at the end of the day are most happy. Codependency is often mistaken for love. The other person is idolized, and the self is lost. Losing myself in an addictive relationship is not something I ever want to experience again. In that disillusionment, I didn't need or want to spend time with anyone else but my partner.

Control is an illusion. Freeing others results in freeing ourselves. Fear that our partner will cheat or abandon us is stressful. Intimacy happens when relationships possess honesty, openness, and mutuality.

Past relationships are behind us. No person has the same qualities and morals as another.

"We come to love not by finding the perfect person, but by learning to see an imperfect person perfectly." - Sam Keen, *To Love and Be Loved*

It takes real courage to love. Love can break us and shatter us to pieces, or it can feel like heaven on earth. It is as critical to your mind and body as is oxygen. To get love and keep love, you have to be active and learn various specific skills. If you seek a partner to share life with, he will not come knocking on your door. Every person in the world is unique. When issues surface for couples, they need to be identified, discussed, and negotiated. I learned this the hard way, but I also learned that it takes both parties. Attempt to understand that your partner's needs are different than yours, respecting and honoring that difference. Many fear the vulnerability that love requires. It is necessary to be brave enough to indulge in self-love, let alone love for others.

If you can endure a two-week vacation with a partner, then you have something exceptional. Vacationing in the mountains is a high priority in the relationship I have with my present husband. Each of us returns to the center of our beings, better able to relax, reconnect and pray together. With more time to talk without the hustle and bustle of daily life, we are reminded of our importance to each other. In learning that if you focus on what is going well, instead of emphasizing what is wrong, there is bound to be greater harmony.

"At this time, somewhere in the world, there is someone would be happy to have you." - Walter Riso

Something I adopted in observing compatible couples is to say *please* and *thank you* not only to my partner but also to everyone. Showing appreciation and respect for your partner is essential. Giving compliments, spending time apart, and performing chores together is good advice for a healthy relationship.

If you are a people pleaser and give too much in relationships, you may have abandonment issues. People with these issues also have trust issues, control others, and stay in unhealthy relationships. They consciously or unconsciously sabotage their romantic connections and move from one unhealthy relationship to another. They may find themselves drawn to people who will treat them poorly and eventually leave them reinforcing their fears and distrust of others.

Most people who sometimes give too much have exceptionally kind hearts and are incredibly caring by nature. Women usually report that they feel as though they give and give and receive little in return. Giving is healthy if you are giving from a full heart and your personal needs are met. We all hope our gifts will be appreciated, and helping others feels great as it brings joy into their lives. But if you feel obligated to give, or have the inability to receive gifts, attention, help from others, or are afraid someone will leave you if you don't give, then you may be in trouble. Giving in the hopes of getting something back can boomerang and leave you feeling insecure.

In my search for a successful relationship, I realized that anyone active in an addiction (sex, drugs, alcohol, love, religion) could not be fully present for me. The addiction is first, and you are second or third. I was persistent in asking Lisa, "Why does he not love me?" She would always reply, "Mary, it's not you!" Then one day, I finally got it!

"At your absolute best, you still won't be good enough for the wrong person. At your worst, you'll still be worth it to the right person." - Karen Salmansohn

I grew considerably after a seven-year on-and-off relationship with an alcoholic. The pain was as great as the growth, as the connection to love was soulful and deep. In *The Secret Language of Relationships* by Gary Goldschneider and Joost Elffers, our personality title was *Between Heart and Head.* I thank his soul for the lessons I needed to learn during our time together. The song, *I Will Survive* by Gloria Gaynor describes a detailed account of the story. The power I gained as a woman was phenomenal!

> *"We don't have to take things so personally. We take things to heart that we have no business taking to heart. For instance, saying, "If you loved me, you wouldn't drink" to an alcoholic makes as much sense as saying, "If you loved me, you wouldn't cough" to someone who has pneumonia. Pneumonia victims will cough until they get appropriate treatment for their illness. Alcoholics will drink until they get the same. When people with a compulsive disorder do whatever it is, they are compelled to do, and they are not saying they don't love you—they are saying they don't love themselves."* - Melody Beattie, *Codependent No More*

Love changes as we change. Scientists have proven that the mind and body change every seven years. I am sure you have heard about the seven-year itch in marriages. If our partner refuses to grow with us or will not accept our changes, couples can grow apart. I believe this is the reason for most breakups. Unlike the song *All You Need Is Love,* sometimes love is not enough.

With relationships come challenges. There are numerous justifications made as to why a relationship is not working. By knowing and understanding ourselves and our fears, we can discover how we can self-sabotage our intimate connections. Do you associate love with pain or believe the more you care, the more you will be hurt? Or do you struggle with feelings of valuing yourself enough to know that you deserve love? By getting to know ourselves, we give ourselves the best chance of finding and maintaining lasting love.

There is no need to feel guilty, disappointed, or hurt, but we do. It takes both partners to do the work. It is hard work with communication and honesty as key ingredients. If my first husband and I could have communicated and discussed the hurtful events in our relationship, maybe we could have preserved the marriage. Intimacy provides an emotional connectedness between two people. When I realized he deserved peace and love just as much as I did, I let him go. I no longer felt guilty or ashamed for the failed relationship, as I called it. I decided to surrender lovingly for both of us. Don't be afraid to love again. Not everyone is your ex.

Life does not happen *to* us; it happens *for* us. People get stressed, looking for explanations of why something happened. Some use the phrase "I should have" a lot. The word *should* is based on the past generating unnecessary guilt and causes us to feel unworthy, shameful, rejected, and feeling like a failure. When someone *shoulds* on you, there is judgment and blame. *Shoulding* is at the center of many relationships power struggles and conflicts.

Could, however, is filled with opportunity and possibility. Try to replace the word should with could whenever you can and notice the difference. I adopted this eleventh commandment for myself, "Thou shalt not should on thyself."

Relationships are like riding a roller coaster. Sometimes you go up, and sometimes you go down. At times, you have to hang on tight, and sometimes you have to get off.

Even if your former partner was selfish, unloving, and you fought a lot, you can still mourn the relationship's loss. According to a study published in the Journal of Neurophysiology, relationship breakups are painful because the part of the brain associated with reward, motivation, and addiction cravings is activated. You may lose your faith in love and never want to feel this way again. Dealing with rejection is painful. But living with someone who is not treating you with love and respect can create many years of suffering. Staying in an emotionally or verbally abusive relationship can have long-lasting effects on your physical and mental health, including chronic pain, depression, or anxiety. Many couples remain in a relationship for fear of being alone or for the sake of the children, adapting to a partner who does not treat them well. Do not ignore that little voice inside your head that tells you, "Something is wrong here."

Gaslighting is a form of emotional abuse that chips away at your confidence by doubting your reality. You may be accused of being stupid, making a big deal out of nothing, and forgetting things. It can make you feel crazy and question your sanity.

"If someone is not treating you with love and respect, it is a gift if they walk away from you. If that person doesn't walk away, you will surely endure many years of suffering with him or her. Walking away may hurt for a while, but your heart will eventually heal.

Then you can choose what you really want. You will find that you don't need to trust others as much as you need to trust yourself to make the right choices." – Don Miguel Ruiz, *The Four Agreements*

Trust me, I know how painfully difficult breakups are, and so is divorce. Divorce is an excruciating process both for the person who is leaving and for the person left behind. It is the death of a relationship that you thought would last until one of you passed on. People who have not been through it, cannot understand how deep and debilitating the pain is. You also hurt and worry about the many changes in your life. You ask yourself, "Where and how will I live? How will I spend weekends and holidays? Can I support myself? How will this affect my children and family?" You will feel guilty crying and feeling like a failure, but know deep down this is the right thing to do to find peace. The pain seems to last forever, but your heart will eventually heal. As a result, you will ultimately recognize how much you have grown by having such an experience. Leaving my husband was the hardest decision I had to make in my life. I realized how many people it would affect. But having the chance to discover the reasons behind my insecurities and heal them was the most beautiful gift I could have ever given myself. It was a rebirth of who I eventually became.

Trust yourself to make the right choices and listen to your body because it will never lie to you. I lived with chronic constipation and sinus headaches for decades. Sinus headaches metaphysically indicate anger towards someone close to you, and constipation is feeling bound up. When I left that relationship, all of these symptoms disappeared. Even though alcohol was not consumed for some time, the *Jekyll/Hyde* personality was always present, and I walked on eggshells for years. The body, mind, and spirit all work together. The mind can play tricks on you, but your intuition and body constantly attempt to tell you the truth.

Another person can bring out the emotion of love we have inside of us. If the love you feel for another is *your* love, how do you know the other person loves you?

The answer is not black and white, but all of us feel and show love differently. There are numerous tell-tale signs; the obvious is hearing the words, "I love you." The other person will desire to be with you, touch you, and look at you. You will be the first one he calls with good news. He will listen and empathize with you, be there for you, giving you compliments. Pay attention to little details like a smile, a hug, or the other person bringing home supper, so you don't have to cook.

" I walk down the street.
There is a deep hole in the sidewalk.
I fall in.
I am lost... I am helpless.
It isn't my fault.
It takes forever to find a way out.

I walk down the same street.
There is a deep hole in the sidewalk.
I pretend I don't see it.
I fall in again.

I can't believe I am in the same place.
But it isn't my fault.
It still takes me a long time to get out.

I walk down the same street.
There is a deep hole in the sidewalk.
I see it is there.
I still fall in. It's a habit.
My eyes are open.
I know where I am.
It is my fault. I get out immediately.

I walk down the same street. "Go
There is a deep hole in the sidewalk. Around."
I walk around it.

I walk down another street."
- Portia Nelson, *There's a Hole in My Sidewalk:*
Romance of Self-Discovery

When I feel like a caged mouse going around and around on a hamster wheel getting nowhere, I suddenly recognize the insanity of it and decide to jump off. It's not always easy to do, but later I can see the silver lining in the clouds. It is difficult to know the *whys* when you are hurting. Sometimes the revelation of why is revealed later.

Even Aristotle believed that things happen today because they have a purpose later on. Everyone in our lives is there for a reason. Everyone in our past has contributed to who we are today. Adopting this philosophy brings the gift of acceptance. It's a great coping mechanism for a life we cannot always control. Trust that when one door closes, another will open.

Whether we like it or not, situations are constantly changing in our lives, but they never remain the same for long. The opportunity to grow is a continuous process in our lives. People can come into our lives to remind us of what matters most. They may awaken us, help us find our strength, or aid us physically, emotionally, or spiritually. When their work is done, they will bring the relationship to an end without any wrongdoing. They may say something, do something, die, walk away, or act out, forcing you to make a decision. Then it will be time to move on. Believing and trusting that we have planned out everything in our life with our guides certainly makes life more tolerable. It is all for our greatest good; understanding the Universe knows what is best for us. Trust in God and trust in the process.

"People come into your life for a reason, a season, or a lifetime. When you figure out which one it is, you will know what to do for each person." - Author Unknown

Lessons accompanied each of my love relationships, bringing a realization that I deserved better. Relationships improved as self-esteem increased. Again, like attracts like. Our surroundings give us clues to our inner state.

Children come into this world with two basic emotional needs, the need to feel loved, and the need for positive self-esteem. The need for love begins at birth. The loving care of feeding as well as comforting the child builds trust, making them feel safe. As children grow, the need continues with positive feedback and loving support. Spending time with your children, responding to questions, taking an interest in their everyday affairs, and letting them know that what they *did* is unacceptable, not who they are. Separating the action from the person is essential. Smiling, hugs, kisses, and saying, "I love you" is just as necessary as validating their feelings. Praise enhances good self-esteem and approval. Children form an image of themselves by hearing your words and observing your actions. Your greatest challenge as a parent is for your child to feel good about himself. Avoid criticism, comparisons, and negative labels. Verbal abuse like name-calling, teasing, shaming, insulting, comparing, and criticizing is as harmful as physical abuse. Words can hurt as hard as a fist. When children are exposed to verbal abuse or violence, it weakens their sense of self-worth and prepares the way for hopelessness.

Apologizing to your child and admitting fault helps to ward off perfection, emphasizing that we are all here to learn and grow even in adulthood. A parent's role is to provide the necessary love and guidance, thereby helping your child mature into a healthy adult who will contribute constructively to society. We prepare them for the world by teaching values, giving direction, establishing and imposing rules, using discipline and setting limits, following through with consequences, as well as holding them accountable for their behaviors.

Parenting is the most important job you will ever have. I believe most of us did the best we could as parents with the knowledge, understanding, and awareness we had at that time. But many of our problems have genetic roots, and it is impossible to control the environment a child grows up in. A child's brain works in a way where they learn automatically from observing. If a parent can understand and manage their behavior, it teaches the child to do the same. To model is to teach. Everyone remembers hearing the phrase, "Do as I say, and not as I do." With or without awareness, children are picking up their attitudes, feelings, and sense of values. The importance of being in control of yourself is critical to good parenting.

I vowed to break this cycle of dysfunction in my immediate family. I joined the *Plymouth County Council for the Prevention of Child Abuse and Neglect,* representing our county in the state of Iowa. I enrolled in grant writing courses to submit funding for prevention programs. Funding was granted, and we were informed that our county was in dire need of keeping families together. Too many children were being taken from their parents and placed in foster care.

As coordinator and instructor, I hired teachers, including Lisa and my daughter, and others, to teach the *Parent Education Nurturing Program* by Dr. Stephen J. Bavolek. Parents and their children were divided into classes and presented with a study program using books, videos, discussions, handouts, and assessments. Families received appropriate age expectation charts for each child. Unrealistic age expectations of children cause a lot of unneeded stress for both parents and children.

The program's long-term goal was to lower the rate of teen pregnancies; reduce juvenile delinquency, drug, and alcohol abuse, thereby reducing the multi-generational cycle of abuse and neglect in families.

Alternatives to spanking were introduced, including timeouts, ignoring, rewards and consequences, and taking away privileges. New skills were proposed, like praising and empowering. Separating the child's actions is critical; informing them that what they *did* was unacceptable, rather than *who they are* is deficient. The roadblocks facing parents were that new techniques took more time, and consistency was vital.

A two-hour class included a break with snacks and an interactive game for all family members. Games included *Duck-Duck-Grey-Duck*, *Musical Chairs*, and *London Bridge*. Some parents were too uncomfortable to participate, finding it difficult to allow their inner child to come out to play.

Until I moved to another state, two fifteen-week programs were offered in the county annually for twelve years. The court system ordered some families to enroll, but most were registered voluntarily, with classes being free of charge.

There were a few parents who could not accept the nurturing concept versus spanking. I recall one father stating that he was repeatedly disciplined as a child with a bat, insisting he always deserved it. He was obese and an alcoholic. His wife divorced him a year later, after enrolling in a co-dependency group. After receiving gastric bypass surgery, he continued drinking, regaining his lost weight.

When attending a state conference, I met and participated in a workshop with the program's author. Dr. Bavolek is a recognized leader in child abuse and neglect prevention treatment and parent education. In the past thirty-five years, he has conducted extensive research, published numerous books, and conducted hundreds of workshops. Dr. Bavolek has received numerous international, state, and local awards for his work. As president of Family Development Resource, Inc. and executive director of Family Nurturing Centers International, he continues his mission to educate and improve families.

In his book *Homecoming*, John Bradshaw explains how we can learn to nurture that wounded inner child offering ourselves the proper parenting we needed and longed for. By exploring each developmental stage's unfinished business, it is possible to break away from destructive family rules freeing ourselves to live responsibly in the present. Our inner child can then become a vitality source, enabling us to discover new joy and inner peace.

I was passionate and motivated to teach families how to nurture one another and learn less aggressive forms of discipline. My children were already adults, but the information and education I received from this program were impressive.

The primary task of parenting is to raise healthy, happy, independent, confident human beings capable of making this world a better place with their presence and contributions to society. We learn how to parent from our parents. What was passed on from generation to generation was not always positive, nurturing, or effective. Parenting is the most important job you will ever have, and is the most challenging, demanding, stressful, and rewarding career in the world.

All of us think that if we paid more attention, had a healthier marriage, or worked less, our kids would not have the issues they are living with today. If we had the knowledge, wisdom, and understanding that we have in this present moment, their childhoods might have been more fulfilling. I taught my children many things passed on from generation to generation that simply are not true. I was at an age when I was unable to think for myself. Attempt to understand and forgive yourself, realizing you did the best you could at that time and in those circumstances. We cannot undo the past, but we can give our children now what they need from us. Parenting is a lifetime relationship, and it's never too late to be a better parent. You can start today and give the love you have now and grow together with your child. Maya Angelou states it best," When you know better, you know better."

"Children will not remember you for the material things you provided but for the feeling that you cherished them." – Richard L. Evans

CHAPTER 5

GOD, LOVE, AND SPIRITUALITY

"Happiness is when what you think, what you say, and what you do are in harmony."
- Mahatma Gandhi

A s a fervent Catholic for forty-six years, I attended parochial school from first grade until graduation, attending mass six days a week. There were two Catholic churches on opposite sides of town. St. Joseph is located across town, where I attended school. I walked six blocks to St. James, the west church, each morning, having to attend mass to get a ride on the bus to school. The bus driver would not let us on the bus unless we were seen coming out of the church after mass. One day I arrived late, and the driver saw me walking up the sidewalk, and refused to let me board the bus. I walked back home, and my mother drove me to school. This scenario was the typical rigidity of Catholicism.

In high school, dresses were mandatory for girls. Our family was poor, and I owned three dresses. My favorite was an A-line printed dress. I created two jumpers in my high school sewing class. Wearing different blouses underneath gave them a few different looks. Some girls were starting to wear expensive nylons instead of bobby socks. This created a greater sense of not fitting in for me, feeling even more alienated and different. Students attending Catholic schools were considered wealthy, as tuition was expensive. I don't know how mom afforded it financially, but it must have been very important to her that I attended a Catholic school.

I received all the necessary sacraments in the appropriate, timely manner and voluntarily taught CCD (Confraternity to Christian Doctrine) to third graders for ten years while in my twenties. If the roads were icy, I had to try to get to mass to avoid a mortal sin on my soul. If I died with mortal sin, I would go to hell for eternity. However, if I died with venial sin, I would have to endure the emptiness and loneliness of purgatory.

Teachings in this era articulated that everyone is imperfect and born in sin, instilling feelings of inadequacy in children. I was born in the image and likeness of God, yet I carried the sin of Adam and Eve. And so, I modeled the saints whose heavenly reward was almost guaranteed. Sainthood meant living a life of poverty and selflessness. I remember my first confession at age seven, feeling nervous and scared. After confessing that I disobeyed my parents ten times, the priest replied, "No, it was twenty times." I feared to burn in the fires of hell for eternity; therefore, my goal in life was to earn a heavenly reward. But I didn't think I had much of a chance, as only a handful make it there, but I was certainly going to try.

I now call myself a "recovering Catholic." This term first came into use in the 1980s. It is used by former practicing Catholics where Catholicism has negatively influenced their lives. Catholic upbringing had both positive and negative aspects. The positive influence was developing an excellent moral code as well as a healthy conscience. However, religious teachings were based on fear, creating a child ridden with guilt who had no right to question this teaching. Continually striving for perfection burdens the spirit with anxiety, stress, and worry. It was necessary to relearn, rethink and reprogram myself from childhood abuse and neglect, and the guilt-driven teachings of the Catholic church.

Thoughts of good or bad, right or wrong, lead to passing judgment on yourself as well as others. In striving to be perfect, we tend to compare ourselves to others feeling *less than.*

"Comparison making is one of the major ways that one continues to shame oneself internally. One continues to do to oneself on the inside what was done on the outside." - John Bradshaw

Striving to be perfect sets high standards for ourselves and others that cannot be reached. We criticize ourselves relentlessly when mistakes (lessons) are made, viewing ourselves as inadequate rather than having an opportunity for learning a lesson. If we base our self-worth on actions, achievements, or what others think of us, we will never feel good enough.

"Perfectionism flows from the core of toxic shame. Perfectionists never know how much is good enough. Perfectionism is learned when one is valued only for "doing." When parental acceptance and love

are dependent upon performance, perfectionism is created. The performance is always related to what is outside the self. The child is taught to strive onward. There is never a place to rest and have inner joy and satisfaction. And no matter how hard one tries or how well one does, one never measures up. Not measuring up is translated into a comparison of good versus bad, better versus worse. Good and bad lead to moralizing and judgmentalism." - John Bradshaw

OCD (obsessive-compulsive disorder) is a pattern of thoughts and fears that lead to repetitive behaviors. There is a drive to perform compulsive acts to try to ease worry and stress. It is also a way to try to control life and is a lifelong disorder. Stressful life events and family history contribute to this condition. OCD usually begins in the teen or young adult years of life.

I was a checker. My favorite number is four, and so I checked everything four times. It could take forty-five minutes for me to get into bed at night. I drove myself crazy, checking the doors, stove, and my children's breathing as they slept.

After working through personal fears (especially the fears I learned through Catholicism), the OCD diminished significantly. Now, when it uncovers its ugly head, I ask myself, "What exactly am I worried about?" I view it as a coping mechanism that can create and reduce fear and worry. Symptoms worsen with stress. I talk to my inner child, reassuring her that everything is OK and that there is nothing to fear but fear itself. I still develop unwanted thoughts that cause stress and anxiety. I use prayer, EFT, self-talk, and affirmations to help.

When self-awareness increased, beliefs also changed. Coming from a religious mentality of fear, sin, and judgment that instilled inner shame and guilt, I searched for a loving God.

"It is my fundamental conviction that compassion (the natural capacity of the human heart to feel concern for and connection with another being) constitutes a basic aspect of our nature shared by all human beings, as well as being the foundation of our happiness." - Dalai Lama

Love and compassion are a common thread in all religions. They may differ in their metaphysical views, but all have moral ethics. Religiously unaffiliated and Christian adults also believe in New Age concepts such as reincarnation, astrology, psychics, and the presence of spiritual energy in physical objects like the sun, mountains, or trees. Most of us believe in the possibility and potential that there is something greater than ourselves.

New Age focuses on individualism, open-mindedness, and spiritualism, tracing Eastern religious customs like Hinduism, Buddhism, and other ancient spiritual traditions. Practices include psychic readings, yoga, meditation, tarot cards, alternative bodywork, including chiropractic and massage. Natural health encompasses God-given herbs, ingesting organic foods, using homeopathy, and aromatherapy. Aspirin is derived from the willow bark tree, and its use travels back to over 3,500 years ago.

Native American culture has always captivated me with their practices of ceremonies, rituals, dances, face painting, chanting, and honoring the Great Spirit. I incredibly enjoy attending the Elk Fest in Estes Park, Colorado annually, noting the storytelling, flute playing, community interaction, mediation, and dancing by Apache Danny Many Horses. Numerous tribes are invited to demonstrate their particular traditional tribal dances filling your spirit with respect for Mother Earth and the sanctity of life.

Herbs such as boneset, wild black cherry, dogwood, willow bark, and sage were some of the many medicinal remedies. All of us came from nature, and all of us will return to nature. God is nature. Why would nature *not* be a part of spirituality?

"Everything on the earth has a purpose, every disease an herb to cure it, and every person a mission. This is the Indian theory of existence." - Mourning Dove (Salish) 1888-1936

The Laws of the Universe govern this entire universe, constantly working with us. These laws continuously rule our existence, whether aware of them or not. For over 5,000 years in mystical teachings from Ancient Egypt, Ancient Greece, and Ancient India, these people intuitively understood and taught that everything operates with energy, frequencies, and vibration. Some of these laws are immutable, meaning; they are profound and eternal laws that can't be changed or transcended, but they can be worked with. The mutable laws are impermanent, which means that they can be used in this way to create our realities better.

Learning to transcend mutable laws, we can use them to create the life we desire consciously. These laws are about mastering your life with joy and love. What happens in our lives is the causation of our actions and thoughts. The Twelve Spiritual Laws of the Universe can teach us about happiness, well-being, and success. By understanding and abiding by the Universal Laws of Nature, you can avoid struggle, pain, resistance, and a lack of purpose. Whether you believe in these laws or not, these fundamental truths influence our everyday lives. Whether Christian or not, these common-sense laws can influence you, and your awareness of them can lead to positive changes in your life. They are as follows:

1. Law of Divine Oneness: Created from the same Divine Source, we are part of everything and everyone. By showing more acceptance with compassion towards others, we can apply this law. Everything is connected to everything else. We are all One.

2. Law of Vibration: With high-powered microscopes, we would see that everything is vibrating and constantly moving. This also applies to our frequency of thoughts and actions. Good vibes attract good experiences and vice versa. The sounds of thoughts have their vibration as well.

3. Law of Correspondence: Our reality is a mirror of what's happening inside us. If fear and chaos are within, fear and chaos are in our life. If peace and love are within, our life is calm, and we feel grounded.

As above, so below. The principles and laws of physics that govern the non-physical world energy, such as the vibration of light and motion, have similar regulations in the metaphysical world.

4. Law of Attraction: Like attracts like, and you get what you think about and focus on. This law is similar to the Law of Vibration. If you want more love in your life, give more love to yourself and others. Everyone creates things, events, and people that come into our lives through our thoughts, feelings, words, and actions.

5. Law of Inspired Action: Action is needed to accomplish something. To manifest anything on earth, we must engage in acts that support our thoughts, dreams, words, and emotions. Ask for what you want, then let go of the need to control. Pay attention to your thoughts and signs that may lead you to the manifestation of your desires.

6. Law of Perpetual Transmutation of Energy: This law states that on an energetic level, everything in the Universe is constantly changing, evolving, or fluctuating. Every action begins with a thought, and these thoughts have the power to manifest in our physical reality.

7. Law of Cause and Effect: What you put out will come back to you. Maybe not at that moment, but it will with time. The causes are the decisions we make and the actions we take. This creates predictable and specific effects that we are now experiencing in our

lives. Nothing happens by chance. We reap what we sow. Karma is not punishment, but is an educational lifestyle that promotes positive thinking and actions. To receive happiness, peace, and love; one must *be* happy, peaceful, and loving.

8. Law of Compensation: You will always be compensated for your efforts, actions, and for your contributions; however much or however little. Compensation is a cause and effect applied to blessings and abundance which is provided for us. Our deeds' physical effects are given to us in gifts, friendships, money, and blessings.

9. Law of Relativity: Everyone is inclined to compare things in our world, but in reality, everything is neutral. Meaning is merely about perspective and perception. Each person has the opportunity to strengthen their life within. This can happen through challenges, problems, and tests. When we remain connected to our hearts in solving problems, everything is put into perspective. My mother always said, "there is always someone, somewhere who has it worse."

10. Law of Polarity: To explore and experience life to the fullest, we need to be familiar with both spectrums. How can you know success without knowing failure? How can you appreciate health unless you have known sickness? Everything in life has an opposite. We can transform undesirable thoughts by focusing on the positive.

11. Law of Rhythm: The Universe is full of movement and flow. It is the dance of life. The Law of Rhythm is at work continuously, with good times and bad times, successes and failures, seasons changing, markets rising and falling, and growing and dying. Try to flow with the cycles and patterns, as they will always be a part of life.

12. Law of Gender: Everyone holds both gender principles and positive and negative poles inside our body and consciousness (Yin and Yang). Every male has the components of female energy within his body and in his Light Body, and every female has the elements of male energy in her body and her light body. With both energies, we co-create with the Universe. From the microscopic levels of subatomic particles moving up the scale to the planets, stars, and solar systems, everything is created from the Law of Gender. To accurately comprehend the Law of Gender is to apply it to unity consciousness.

Spirituality, religion, and the Universe Laws all positively affect mental health, enabling us to tolerate stress by creating purpose, forgiveness, and peace. The benefits of religion teach us good morals, inspire us to serve others, provide inner strength, and enlighten us to forgive. As a member of a church or religious organization, there is a sense of community and family.

Being spiritual describes a state of connection to God, nature, and ourselves. When in alignment with our body, mind, and spirit, God/Source/Spirit is both inside and outside our being.

After enduring the dark, lonely tunnel of transformation and healing, my heart was wide open for love and spirituality. Letting go of pain, bitterness, resentments, expectations, blame, resistance, and anger created space, making room for the new.

"I say it is wrong for any religious preacher or teacher to try to place a burden of guilt on anybody by preaching that any person is responsible for the crucifixion of Jesus two thousand years ago. Would God want to trouble the mind, heart, and soul of his children by preaching to them that they are responsible today for the cruel, brutal death of our brother two years ago?" - Nick Bunick, *In God's Truth*

I say," No, not my God." My God is a God of love. He/she does not punish sending his children to hell to burn for eternity. Instead, He teaches us by the Law of Karma. If we caused great pain by teasing someone who was of short stature; we might be short in the next lifetime, experiencing that same pain as empathy is developed.

No religion or belief is the right one. Many paths lead to God/Love. What matters is what is right for you and what fits your soul in this lifetime. All pathways on the road to love are equally valid. Find love within yourself, as you cannot give to others what you do not have within.

"You shall love the Lord, your God, with all your heart and with all your soul and with all your mind. This is the great and first commandment. And a

second is like it: You shall love your neighbor as yourself." - Matthew 11:37-39

We all have a yearning for something beyond physical existence; something that gives purpose, meaning, and value to our lives and the world we live in. Believing in God is a choice and serves a fundamental objective. Beliefs create our reality and our behaviors. The benefits of believing in God build hope, the strength of will, and resilience. For me, God/Universe is energy like the wind. You cannot see it, but you know it's there. You can feel its effects on strength, power, and love. We are all a part of God. "I AM THE I AM." If born in the image and likeness of God, why would we not possess divine essence within ourselves? Why couldn't we co-create with God? This concept makes perfect sense to me.

Life is a journey. Let go of perfection, order, and do something fun for yourself every day. The energy of gratitude will attract more to be thankful for. Happiness begins within. Turn on your favorite music and sing. Activities such as assembling a puzzle with your child, spending more time in nature, and playing with your pet are simple ways to find pleasure and peace. I like to tear apart a flower and discover its intricacy and beauty inside. With age comes more realization that the little things in life mean the most, especially family and good health.

I see God in nature and, most significantly, in the majestic mountains in Colorado. I visit Rocky Mountain National Park each year, experiencing tears of joy when arriving, and tears of sadness when leaving. I know my soul has lived here before because it feels like home. There is a perceivable sense of sitting in the palm of God's hand, nourishing my body, mind, and spirit with a mixture of peace, love, and joy. It is in this sacred place I want my ashes to be scattered. I will then be one with the mountains and God. As John Muir stated, "The mountains are calling, and I must go."

A psychic informed me that I had lived many lives in the mountains. In one life as an Indian squaw, I walked for miles in the hot sun with blistering burnt skin and feet. A skin condition revealed itself to me again in this existence. I was discovered and cared for by a mountain man, and we fell in love. I met him also in this lifetime with familiarity when I looked into his eyes. Eyes are the windows to the soul. We lived together for five years loving and supporting each other as we both learned valuable life lessons.

I always proclaimed that our family was not a family of four, but five, including mom. She accompanied us on vacations, car trips, all holidays, and birthdays. We enjoyed rummage sailing together, and she worked with me as a volunteer at the Christian Needs Center twice a week for many years. Most weekends were spent at our house playing croquet and grilling in the backyard. Winter months included playing various card games and a challenging game of Scrabble together on Sundays. We were both very competitive, becoming ecstatic when composing a two-triple word score. High scores were always recorded to beat in future challenges. I can still hear her laughing while watching television shows like *Two and a Half Men* and *I Love Lucy*. She had a great laugh that was very genuine. When she learned how to use the VCR (she exhausted three of them), she recorded several programs each day, delighting in her acquired knowledge of operating the machine. *Days of Our Lives* was recorded whether she watched it or not. Mom taped educational shows for me, such as *Bear Grylls, John Bradshaw,* and *John Edward.*

As a fervent Catholic, she was open-minded to all possibilities, and discussions included the possibility of aliens and communicating with those on the other side. Our conversations were exhilarating as nothing was off the charts. Nothing surprised, Mom! She communicated with me a lot after her departure, primarily through the Healing with the Angels angel cards, and continues to visit me in dreams several times a week for the past eleven years.

Mom is remembered for her famous taverns and homemade apple pie. Our family honors her by sharing a meal consisting of Grandma's taverns, chips, and dip. Only my son has come close to her recipe, as no one can add that missing special ingredient of Grandma's love.

The first summer after mom's transition, I made my annual visit to Estes Park, Colorado. Visiting there renews my soul, recapturing the tranquility and simplicity of life. Being submerged in nature brings a sense of happiness, peace, and contentment. As an internal gift to our soul, it is the closest feeling in relating to God or higher energy.

I asked mom," If there is anything you can do to manifest a bear sighting, I would be so grateful." I searched for bears on each visit for thirty-four years. On the final day of the vacation, my request was granted. While driving down the mountain on Hi-Way 34, on Big Thompson from Estes to Drake; I saw a large black bear on the side of the road, eating chicken from a black plastic garbage bag. She dragged the bag from the overturned trash container from the restaurant across the street. I screamed," Oh my God, oh my God," making a U-turn quickly. Her three cubs were in a nearby tree playing as she ate. We took many photos keeping a safe distance as she ate. I sobbed with tears of joy, astonished and grateful that Mom would and could do that for me.

A month before making that trip, I made up a story for my grandchildren while laying them down for an afternoon nap. The story included a black bear who had wandered into town eating chicken bones from the trash on a family's back porch.

But wait, this gets even more interesting! Shortly after arriving home from this magical trip, my heart felt heavy missing mom, so I pulled out a box of old photos from the closet. As I opened the cardboard box's flaps, the photo laying on top was an image of mom smiling at me, posing with a black bear. She had the most significant and brightest smile I have ever seen on her face. I snapped that photo of her while we were all on vacation in Colorado about thirty years ago. Unable to encounter a live bear on our trip, she posed next to a bear sculpture in a general store. I completely forgot about taking this photo. Grateful for the communication she blessed me with, I sobbed with delight. Rocky Mountain National Park will be where my ashes are scattered as it is undoubtedly a magical place.

On the tenth anniversary of mom's transition, I awoke after dreaming of mom and bears at the very hour of her passing. Her spirit continues to let me know that she is still with me.

CHAPTER 6

♡

UNIVERSAL LAWS IN OVERDRIVE

"By now, it seems clear that we are all living through a major turning point in history, one that will be studied for years to come. Future textbook authors will write entries on the year 2020, revise them, and revise them so some more with each new edition."
- The Atlantic

D isorder and complete confusion describe the year 2020. Life was a never-ending vicious circle of emotions from sadness to hope, denial to acceptance, and fear to courage. All of us witnessed sequential changes beginning with legendary basketball player Kobe Bryant and his daughter's accidental deaths, Prince Harry and Meghan's departure from the Royal family, the global stock market crash, the impeachment and acquittal of President Donald Trump, the sentencing of former movie producer Harvey Weinstein for sex crimes, the COVID-19 pandemic, the devastating fires in Australia, Colorado, and California, killer murder hornets arriving in our country, the Black Lives Matter movement with protests and riots, and the

COVID-19 vaccine rollout. This year will never be forgotten.

Black Lives Matter (BLM) is a political and social movement protesting police brutality incidents, and all racially motivated violence against Black people. The movement began in July 2013, after George Zimmerman's acquittal in the African American teen Trayvon Martin's shooting death. The movement gained more attention after the George Floyd incident in 2020. George Floyd died after a police officer continued to hold his knee on George's neck for almost nine minutes, even after Mr. Floyd stated he could not breathe.

Anger was evident during the Black Lives Matter riots. People used criticism and sarcasm and found faults in others. I could feel the tension in Facebook postings. Many were posting fake news mixed with angry and contemptuous comments with this form of communication of not being face to face. It took a toll on friendships and even divided families. These are unhealthy ways of expressing anger.

The pandemic certainly caused fear, pain, and frustration, which are at the roots of anger. Many lost their jobs and were worried about paying the rent, keeping the electricity on, and feeding their families. Those who depended on food banks for the first time felt humiliated. Angry people look for ways to channel their anger. Some responded by punching, kicking, breaking things, and hurting other people.

We usually get angry at someone because of what they did. Hate involves the whole aspect of the person or group. Often revenge is part of hate when someone wants to cause the same pain to another as they caused to them. People who hate lack self-compassion and empathy for others. If we are OK with ourselves, responding to others will include empathy for them. Living in a culture that promotes violence and competition teaches us an eagerness to fight, rather than resolving conflict peacefully.

A half a million people turned out in protest of George Floyd's murder in nearly 550 places across the United States. Riots and protests ravaged most parts of the nation from May to August. Turnouts ranged from dozens to tens of thousands in about 250 small towns and cities. With this as well as the pandemic, tensions were high. People were angry about in-person classes for their children, those not abiding by the latest public health guidelines, workers being forced to work at home or losing their jobs, and all the unknown about the virus.

Demonstrators came out nightly, and protesting intensified into rioting. Vandals smashed storefront windows, with looting, violence, and destruction breaking out. Cities imposed curfews to keep people off the streets. Police officers were criticized for using pepper spray, batons, and firing off pepper balls. National guards responded with vast plumes of tear gas, rubber bullets, and flash-bang grenades that created a war zone. Some rioters set small fires, punctured police car tires with spikes, and shined lasers in officers' eyes, pelting them with rocks and frozen water bottles. Fireworks, rocks, bear repellents, ball bearings, and bottles were targeted at officers. According to the Times' analysis, there had been an average of 140 demonstrations per day in 2020.

Justice was finally served. On April 21, 2021, police officer Derek Chauvin was found guilty on three charges second-degree murder, third-degree murder, and manslaughter.

When people are subjected to prejudice, it affects their self-esteem so that they feel less than human. They have no desire to try to improve their lives, and can become angry bullies. This is as damaging to humanity as it is to their growth. It hinders their opportunity to learn, and grow, improving society. Prejudice is never justified.

People were acting psychotic, and society was going mad. Trying to cope with a mysteriously unknown pandemic was enough to endure. These were not normal times. Our lives were being reshaped, but all we could do was surrender and pray. We sensed the Universe was calling out a news flash that it was time to wake up. When humanity and the earth suffer, we learn that it is no longer acceptable to hide behind conscious or unconscious belief systems that no longer serve us. We were all compelled to question where our beliefs and patterns were flawed. Past decisions have undoubtedly impacted our society, which was one of the reasons we were experiencing these unsettling times. This was an opportunity to make changes to ourselves and our world.

"Everyone thinks of changing the world, but no one thinks of changing himself." - Leo Tolstoy

Specific laws govern our Universe. What happens in our lives is the causation of our actions and thoughts. The Laws of the Universe regulate all of creation and are constantly working with us. These laws continuously determine our existence, whether aware of them or not. The Laws of the Universe were compelling us to become enlightened. It was time for each of us to redefine our beliefs and values and explore the root causes of violence, hatred, greed, defiance, narcissism, judgment, lack of trust, and anger.

The Law of Attraction is a law that governs your body and your mind. The principle is that everything that happens to you, whether positive or negative, has been attracted by you. This can be a difficult pill to swallow. How and why would I want to draw this to myself?

First, we need to understand that the unconscious mind is as persuasive as the conscious mind. The most important part of the Law of Attraction is positive thinking, and its foundation is gratitude. Positive thinking requires effort with the right attitude. Replacing fear-based thoughts in a time of uncertainty can be very difficult. It takes mindful daily focus and brain training. This was our daily challenge.

The energy of being grateful sends positive vibes out to the Universe. Like attracts like, so you attract more good things to yourself. It is imperative to focus on what you want, and not what you don't want. In other words, if you think, "I don't want to contract the virus," for example, the Universe will understand, "I want the virus.". To say," I want to remain healthy", is a positive statement. I always thought that the concept of the intelligent Universe not understanding the word *not* or *don't,* was strange. But it's not about the negative; it's about what you are focused on. It is also about asking, believing the reality of your thoughts, and receiving.

Before the pandemic, many things were taken for granted. This is human nature. The epidemic cultivated more appreciation for the little things, such as watching an enjoyable movie on *Netflix*, having delightful neighbors, *Facebook* friends, and driving out to the lake. What I missed the most, was taking the grandchildren to the movies and sharing popcorn. There was always hope that this would end, but it sounded like it was a long time coming. This virus would stick around for a long time as it continued to mutate into other variations.

"The greatest revolution of our generation is the discovery that human beings, by changing the inner attitudes of their minds, can change the outer aspects of their lives." - Williams James

The Law of Cause-and-Effect principle allows us to see life not as a set of random events, but rather as a free choice of thought that can be fashioned to create the life we desire. The causes are the decisions we make and the actions we take. Every decision and action that has been taken, (no matter how small or insignificant), has set into motion the events we are now experiencing in our lives. Because nothing happens by chance or luck; therefore, everything happens for a reason, whether good or bad, as a direct result of the cause you brought about from within yourself.

The First Amendment gives us the right to protest peacefully. But individuals can lose their sense of rationality and follow the crowd. As social beings, we are influenced by others on how to act. There is a desire to be popular and not stick out from the crowd. Evil people can take advantage of a crowds' gullibility, manipulating them into using violence and destruction.

Whether recognized or not, we are constantly choosing the conditions of our lives. We are the authors of our life stories and have the power to co-create with God. Who you were in the past is because your thoughts manifested into that reality. But the good news is that through the power of thought and changing the perspective of your world, you can manifest a new reality. With our God-given free choice, we can choose to change our thoughts about our world, events, ourselves, and others. The learned and conditioned psychological patterns that are within us filter our experience of reality. With free choice, we can unlearn thoughts, behaviors, and reactions that keep us from acquiring the life we desire. It is never too late to become a conscious thinker, and turn your life around.

The year 2020 was filled with uncertainty, fear of the unknown, disempowerment, and loneliness. Christians predicted the end of the world, and the second coming of Christ, and were caught up in the fear trap.

"Fear is a vital response to physical and emotional danger – if we didn't feel it, we couldn't protect ourselves from legitimate threats." - Psychology Today

But fear can become our worst enemy, causing us to experience extreme anxiety and depression.

Emotional exhaustion slowly built up. Stress just keeps coming and coming, pushing many to feel worn out, drained, irritable and trapped. Humanity had no control and did not know what to expect next. Emotional symptoms included anxiety, depression, hopelessness, as well as lack of motivation. Fatigue, muscle aches, and lack of appetite were some symptoms that showed up physically. For me, it was depression and insomnia.

We learned to practice letting go of living from day to day, appreciating each other, and viewing this as an opportunity to grow and learn. Rather than focusing on fear, the goal was to avoid negative self-talk and thoughts, find support from friends, family, and support helplines during the pandemic. As I noticed more separation in humanity (the failure to address global warming, the division of our government, politics, and racism), I knew the world needed some rehabilitation. The division between *us and them* produces more anger and pain. When the rioting began, I asked myself, "Where is all of this anger coming from?" I knew the answer was a lack of love and compassion. This thought inspired the writing of *Breaking the Chains That Bind You*. We can only bestow on others the degree of love that is inside of us. My writing aims to inspire growth in others, empowering them to become their authentic selves. Your authentic self is you at your deepest core.

Imagine how different our world would be if each of us would take the time for self-reflection. When analyzing our childhoods and resolving any core issues that require healing, the reward will be increased love for ourselves and others. This is how to recondition this world; one person at a time.

"Love is the greatest manifestation of God one can give to another, and one can receive from another. If every one of us in the world embraced love, we would not have wars; we would not have prisons; we would not have hungry children; we would not have abused women, for none of these things could exist in a world filled with love." - Nick Bunick, *In God's Truth*

The Law of Correspondence tells us there is harmony, agreement, and correspondence between the physical, mental and spiritual realms. "As above, so below; as below, so above." This means that our outer world is a reflection of our inner world, showing us that our current reality mirrors what is going on inside of us. If we are facing inner turmoil and troubles, that will also manifest in our outer world. However, if we are balanced, happy, and at peace within ourselves, then that is also what we will be experiencing in our outer world. This is a Universal Truth. Each of us must take responsibility for what is currently in our lives. Life requires our participation and does not just happen by itself.

"When you change the way you look at things, the things you look at change." - Wayne Dyer

If you can do the inner work and focus on finding inner peace, joy, and happiness without the need for external fulfillment, you will find yourself seeing the world in a whole new, beautiful light. When you are aligned within, the world around you will align perfectly, too.

A lot of us were feeling stress, anxiety, and frustration during the pandemic as we faced uncertainty. The word meditation is widely used, but mindful meditation is the most common practice. It merely means that we are purposely paying attention to the present moment. I like to close my eyes and listen to the various sounds I hear, counting them. This practice slows our heart rate, lowers our blood pressure, calms us, centering us in the now. Walking in nature and absorbing a tree's beauty, a squirrel, a lake, is also a form of meditation that grounds us. I repeatedly told my husband that I did not feel grounded after six months into the pandemic. I can only recall a few times in my life when I felt that way. I needed a break from the news and the repetition of doing the same thing day after day. So, we went camping. Earth is the element of our planet, and a lack of nature may lead any person to have trouble grounding themselves. Earth signs have a unique relationship to nature. Earth signs include *Taurus, Virgo,* and *Capricorn.* Realizing this, I took walks in the forest, discovering different colored leaves and pretty pine cones to collect and examine. I crafted pine cone centerpieces for myself and my children. Within a short time, I felt anchored and connected to my center again.

Another way to calm yourself is by using your breath. Breathe in through your nose, deeply filling your abdomen with air, releasing it thoroughly from your mouth until you feel like you have exhaled it all. I like to visualize the stress mixed with the breath as I release it back into the Universe. Occasionally I will ask the Universe to transform my released energy into positive healing energy and give it to someone who needs it the most at that particular time.

It was important to be informed, but listening to the news daily was harmful to our peace of mind. Every day for weeks, the governor, mayor, and the public health director provided updates and reports on local television at the same time each afternoon. When realizing how it affected my anxiety, I limited myself to how often I watched the news.

Focusing on gratitude and prayer was helpful as well. Facebook was full of positive, uplifting posts and quotes. As we instigated hope in one another; we did so to ourselves as well.

The Law of Divine Oneness reminds us that all of us are energetically connected to each other as well as to all things. Everything that exists, seen and unseen, is connected, inseparable from each other to a field of divine oneness. Everything is energy, so the thoughts we think, the words we speak, and the actions we take impact us individually and collectively. Televisions blaring with fear-filled coronavirus news toxified our homes and minds with negativity, regardless if anyone was watching it or not. It was understood that we were in this pandemic together with the whole world. COVID-19 did not discriminate. Every action we take has a ripple effect and impacts the collective consciousness of all. We learned to shift our consciousness from fear to hope. The greeting namaste describes this best." When you are in that place in you, and I am in that place in me; then we are One." Everyone comes from the same Source energy. When we heal some of our pain, we heal some of the world's pain. When we focus on healing some of the world's pain, we are recovering some of our pain, knowing that we are not separate from anyone or anything. We learned to be compassionate with others who have lost loved ones from the virus.

"A human being is a part of the whole called by us universe, a part limited in time and space. He experiences himself, his thoughts, and feelings as something separated from the rest, a kind of optical delusion of his consciousness. This delusion is a kind of prison for us, restricting us to our personal desires and affection for a few persons nearest to us. Our task must be to free ourselves from this prison by widening our circle of compassion to embrace all living creatures and the whole of nature in its beauty." - Albert Einstein

We discovered that helping others in need was also a way to help ourselves. Those who were quarantined at home found ways to give back by donating money or supplies or checking in on people who might need support. Every personal contribution was an inspiration to others as well as a contribution to the whole. Volunteering and giving made us feel happier and healthier. It lowered stress, anxiety, boosted our mood, giving us a sense of purpose during this difficult time. We soon learned that this virus was not happening *to* us but *for* us.

The Law of Inspired Action is related to the Law of Attraction, but instead of planned action, it is a gentle nudge that comes from within. Slowing down, getting quiet, and creating space for internal guidance is how to practice this law. With the pandemic, there was no choice. Our need to control and arrange our life forced us to let go. In doing so, we were open to all possibilities knowing we had no control as to future outcomes. We were accustomed to searching the web for information, but there was little to find as no one knew what to expect from this new virus. Our only source of knowledge was the nightly news, and the facts changed daily. Acquiring more details led to overthinking, which led to feeling more overwhelmed and confused. An inspired action isn't a plan of action. It is the guidance we receive to take some sort of action. By listening closely to the voice inside us, we have all the answers we need to make choices and feel confident that we are doing the best for ourselves and our families. The Law of Inspired Action gave us the sense that we should do something. For some, it was the inclination to sew masks, distribute them, listen to less news, spend more time in nature, volunteer their time to help others, etc. It gave us some comfort to be productive and take some action. I did not intend to write a second book. As I was nudged by my guides, this desire to compose appeared unexpectedly without warning, as did *My Journey Finding Love.*

These are only some examples of how a few of these laws were exceedingly active during this time. These twelve Laws of the Universe are working with us and for us at all times. A complete list of the laws will be listed and described in a later chapter.

The coronavirus pandemic was first identified in December 2019 in Wuhan, China, and spread rapidly across one hundred and ninety countries around the world. The symptoms were ever-changing and included fever, chills, cough, shortness of breath, muscle, and body aches, headache, loss of taste or smell, sore throat, congestion, runny nose, nausea, and vomiting. Some experienced no symptoms at all, and millions of lives were lost. People remained infectious for up to two weeks, and everyone in the household was asked to quarantine for that amount of time. Symptoms appeared two to fourteen days after exposure to the virus. The virus spread mainly through the air when people were in close contact with each other.

For those who could not self-isolate and quarantine, the *Center for Disease Control* recommended that everyone wear a face mask or covering in a public setting; keep a social distance of six feet apart; avoid contact with others by washing hands frequently. Wearing a face mask limited exposure to respiratory droplets, preventing those who have the virus from spreading it. Yet, a sizable number of Americans refused to wear a mask in public. People who wouldn't wear a mask saw it as a sign of solidarity, making a stand against authority. Those who did saw it as an act of humanitarianism. Some people did not think the threat was relevant to them, feeling their risk was minimal. At first, the elderly with lowered immune systems with underlying health conditions had the most significant risk of dying. Many who got COVID-19 recovered and did not experience a death in the family after contracting the virus.

While work was underway to develop vaccines, there were lockdowns issued, travel restrictions, with many forced to work from home. Since schools, offices, and libraries were closed, many had to rely on internet access from home. Schools shifted to online learning, but not everyone had access to a personal computer.

Sporting and other events were being canceled, and gatherings of more than six people were not recommended. Many lost their jobs or quit because of the highly contagious virus.

Grocery and department stores, restaurants, and bars offered free pickup service. Younger, healthy individuals volunteered to run errands for those at higher risk, including the elderly, disabled, or housebound. Food banks experienced a higher demand with more people out of work. Items like toilet paper, paper towels, hand sanitizer, bleach, rubbing alcohol, and disinfecting wipes were in short supply. The *Red Cross* was facing dire shortages of blood and plasma as the number of eligible donors had dropped. *Meals on Wheels* experienced a surge in demand to deliver food to older people, as health guidelines recommended that senior citizens stay at home as much as possible.

"You can experience total love in your personal life, for what you give to others is what you get in return. The people who are in our lives come into many different degrees of intimacy to us, from those we live with every day to those who are total strangers we may see once and then never again. Giving love to others should not be confined to one group as opposed to another. It should not be something you turn off and on, like a faucet in a sink, but rather should be an every day, every moment part of your life. It should not be part of you; it should be you." - Nick Bunick, *In God's Truth*

Healthcare workers were exhausted physically as well as emotionally, working double shifts with little sleep. They also faced shortages of PPE (Personal Protection Equipment), such as N95 masks and surgical masks. Essential workers during the pandemic typically included health care, food service, and public transportation, among others.

Stay-at-home orders were in place, with many businesses closing their doors. Family gatherings, weddings, funerals, outdoor activities, and church services were no longer scheduled. Some ignored this warning and conducted their celebrations anyway, creating dozens of COVID-19 transmissions with many deaths in those particular families.

COVID-19 patients were hospitalized in isolation, separated from loved ones, lacking physical contact with family and friends, and dying alone. Doctors and nurses assisted in cell phone and video calls so dying patients could say goodbye to their loved ones. The infection attacked the lungs, filling them with fluid and debris. Ventilators were in short supply, and patients needed them to breathe. As the infection rate rose; so, did the deaths. The virus was as mysterious as it was frightening. Wouldn't it be great if love was the next pandemic?

Funeral homes, mortuaries, and hospitals were overwhelmed with a shortage of beds, personal protective equipment, storage space, staff, embalmers, and directors. Shipping containers usually leased to breweries and restaurants were being rented to ease the overflow of bodies. Los Angeles County had more than one thousand people die from COVID-19 in less than one week. One funeral director advised families to keep the body of their loved one chilled in ice until they could be picked up.

"How could a rich and sophisticated country like the United States of America have the most percentage of deaths and be the hardest-hit country in the world?" we asked. Due to political division, wearing a mask became a political statement rather than a public health measure. With America having just 4% of the world's population, we had 25% of the world's COVID-19 cases and 20% of all COVID-19 deaths as of January 2021.

These were bizarre and extraordinary times with emotions in overdrive for those highly sensitive and willing to own our feelings. With periods of ups and downs, hope and depression, we were all finding a personal way to cope and manage our stress. We tried to be patient, compassionate, and understanding with ourselves and each other, realizing that we were all responding differently. Quarantine and self-isolation can harm anyone's mental health.

Overwhelmed parents and caregivers were homeschooling their children. Children were failing classes, unable to concentrate at home. All were missing hugs, touching, camping, and enjoying weekends at Grandma's and Grandpa's house. I explained to my grandchildren that what was transpiring in the world had never been encountered before in our lifetimes. Children missed their friends, and teachers, and playing outdoors with the neighbors. Public parks were closed because of the easy transmission of the virus by touching the equipment.

My usual schedule of working ten hours per week, socializing, and shopping all came to a halt. I was experiencing shock and an uncertain future. Movies that I viewed as a young adult, such as *Contagion, Outbreak, Carriers, Quarantine,* and *Virus,* were becoming a reality!

Eating is my coping mechanism for added stress, and I was craving the carbs. I thought I might as well enjoy these final days eating some cake and pasta, so I gained weight, which only added to my frustration. I used EFT, Reiki, and listened to calming meditations, but the daily news counteracted the effects. It made good sense to listen to the news as each day provided more information on this strange virus. I tried to balance listening to enough news to keep informed but not obsess about it. It is not good for the body, mind, and spirit to be on high alert at all times. It will eventually wear you down emotionally as well as physically.

After eight months of this insanity; I finally lost it one day, experiencing an emotional outburst of judgment and anger. Fear, pain, and frustration are common roots of anger. Holding anger in can be unhealthy for your mental health. It can cause increased blood pressure, increased heart rate, and restlessness leading to irregular sleeping patterns, anxiety, and eating disorders. The need to be right may affirm and inflate our sense of worth, but it ruins our relationships, obstructs our mindfulness, and destroys our instinct to learn and grow. To judge and verbally attack another is wrong. It not only hurts them, but damages your self-esteem. You later have to evaluate the damage you caused to yourself and others and make amends. But like any life lesson, there is an opportunity to learn from it. The day you stop blaming others is the day you discover who you are. Blaming others is easy, but owning up to your shortcomings demonstrates maturity, responsibility, accountability, and integrity. Even with many apologies, forgiveness was slow to come. Many were taken by surprise that *peacelady* also carried a bad wolf on one shoulder.

Mental health experts raised concerns about the effect that the pandemic was having on the population's mental health. Top problems include long-term isolation, increased rates of depression, trauma, job loss, anxiety, food and substance use disorders, and suicide. People with mental illness and addictions had limited access to supportive resources. Numerous hotlines were finally set up for those who had questions about the virus and those with mental health problems.

Positive human touch is an integral part of human interaction. Whether it's a warm embrace, a reassuring hand on the shoulder, or one arm linked through another; physical contact is a large part of how we show concern and establish camaraderie with friends and loved ones. Touch also helps regulate our digestion and sleep, boosting our immune systems. People are wired to connect with other people on a basic physical level. To deny that is to deprive ourselves of some of life's greatest joys and deepest comforts. And so, this was the new normal. Many tolerated over a year without touching. Touch deprivation can lead to health issues like depression and anxiety. With the elderly, the hunger for touch is stronger than ever. Families with residents in nursing homes were restricted from visiting their loved ones, and many would gather outside their nursing room windows to connect with them. Physical touch is a fundamental part of being human. We yearn to feel needed. When my children dropped off an item at our home, I asked if I could hug their back. The need to feel them was overwhelming. Thank God I had my partner to tolerate this difficult time. Psychologists are concerned that the lack of touch may have a long-term negative impact on our well-being.

Touch is the mother of all senses building connectedness and signals safety and trust. Research has shown that it takes eight to ten meaningful touches a day to maintain physical and emotional health. When a romantic partner places their hands on us, we experience a surge in the hormone oxytocin, often called the love hormone. This happens in the brain, which maintains deep attachment feelings. When meeting and greeting others, people normally shake hands, kiss, or hug depending on the relationship they have with the other person. Touch therapy or massage therapy is not just good for our muscles. It's good for our entire physical and mental health.

Experts point out that there could be positive effects to the new normal if people rethink their priorities, find creative solutions to problems, and develop a more profound sense of empathy and charitableness. I believe the year 2020 has unified us in many ways. Society gained an increased sense of pride and commitment. Vaccines rolled out in record time with (otherwise competitive) pharmaceutical companies working together for the common good. Because of this pandemic, we humans have grown to become more compassionate to the needs of our neighbors, relatives, friends, and ourselves.

The first vaccination for COVID-19 became available in mid-December of 2020. In September of

2021, 53.4% of Americans were fully vaccinated. Booster shots were suggested after eight months of receiving the last vaccination. With viruses constantly changing through mutation, the Delta, Alpha, Gamma, and Beta variants were identified, making the virus twice as contagious with a higher increase in hospitalization and death. This virus was not going to "suddenly disappear."

CHAPTER 7

THE UNLIMITED POWER OF THOUGHT

"If we are willing to let go of our illness, then
we have to let go of the attitudes that brought
about the illness because disease is an
expression of one's attitude and habitual
ways of looking at things. Love restores inner
harmony and every cell in your body is
receptive to the natural state of health."
- David R. Hawkins, MD, Ph.D.

The Law of Correspondence is one of the most critical Universal Laws we know of. It tells us that our current reality is a mirror of what is going on inside us. And so, be mindful of what you are thinking about. Be the watcher of your thoughts and emotions and be honest with yourself in what you see without judgment. Ask yourself how your thoughts are causing, creating, and maintaining your current life circumstances. Your thoughts are energy, force, and frequency. The ability to manage your thoughts is the cornerstone of a successful life.

It is well known that our thoughts can influence our bodies. Stress can worsen illness; fear increases chemicals that induce fight or flight, and thoughts can create muscle contractions. If you ever got sick before an interview, developed a headache after an argument, or bit your nails while watching a scary movie, you know what I am talking about. Thoughts influence the neurotransmitters in your brain, and whenever you have a thought, there is a corresponding chemical reaction in your mind and body as a result. It is essential to recognize this because it confirms that what you think can affect how you feel. If you are feeling bad, you can transform that by changing how you think.

Pay attention to your thoughts becoming aware of triggers and patterns. Buddha states," Thoughts become words. Words become actions. Actions become habits. Habits become character. Watch your character. It becomes your destiny." Maybe each time you get stuck in traffic, you think and react the same way. By choosing to think differently and feeding your brain atypical information, you can program your brain to begin thinking the way you would like it to. Talking to yourself can work wonders in keeping your thoughts positive, and creates calmness. Instead of cursing and being flustered, you can tell yourself that this is an excellent time to call a friend or clean out the glove box.

Take responsibility for what you think. Everything begins with a thought, and the power of your thoughts can create negative or positive emotional states. Thoughts create reality. This book started with a thought that passed through my mind. Our thoughts manifest and grow with interest, attention, and enthusiasm. Our emotions generate thoughts, with magnetic energy attached to them. As our emotions send out high-frequency vibrations such as joy, anything in that vibration is attracted to us. It is the same with lower vibrations like fear, worry, and guilt. Internal negative thoughts create an outer world filled with chaos and hardship. If your life feels unfulfilled, unhappy, and unmanageable, it is because of how you are on the inside. We are like walking magnets pulling into our world anything that is playing on the same frequency. Like attracts like. This is the power of manifestation. When you focus on creating the kind of life and relationships that you desire, you will naturally bring fulfillment, satisfaction, and happiness into your life. To succeed, we must shift our beliefs and thinking. Everyone has the choice to interpret their world differently and change the patterns of their thinking. What you feel and how you react to something is always up to you. Nobody can hurt you without your permission.

"Whether you think you can, or you think you can't-you're right." - Henry Ford

The only person we can change is ourselves. Not only is it not our job to change another, but it is also up to each person to decide if they want to improve their lives or not. It has to come from within, with a desire. All we can do is offer advice, lead by our example, and inspire others. When the time is right, they will remember our words.

Manifest change with your thoughts' power by visualizations, affirmations, by keeping your thoughts and words positive. In realizing that our thoughts create our world, there are numerous ways to change a negative thought. When a feeling of fear comes up for me, I visualize a cancel sign, and repeat, *cancel, cancel,*

cancel. You can also shift your thinking to gratitude by counting ten joys and blessings you are grateful for. Realize that you cannot change others; you can only change yourself and how you react to others. Changing the world begins with changing yourself. Changing how you think will change how you feel and affect the actions that you take. Imagine a world if each of us would practice this.

I replace negative thoughts with a heart-warming vision of a mountain scene at the top of *Rocky Mountain National Park,* watching the marmots as they play on the rocks. Replace the thoughts you want to discard and imagine a face or a scene that makes you happy. Making your brain work for you is the key to making changes in your life.

Affirmations are powerful. Affirmations force your mind to think differently. Constructive affirmations make us feel better about ourselves. Like mantras, they have a spiritual and sacred force to them. Keep your affirmations positive, stating them as if they already have manifested. Affirmations reprogram your subconscious mind with new beliefs. A recording with your voice is more effective, as your conscious mind is communicating with your subconscious and your inner child. Some say it takes twenty-one consecutive days to form a habit. I believe it takes much longer to change a negative thought or concept to a positive one, especially if you are told the same thing every day for many years.

Children think parents are gods who know everything. If you call your child dumb, stupid, or selfish, they will believe you. What we believe about ourselves is usually determined by what we were told as children. Behaviors, decisions, and actions are based on self-esteem and self-concept. Ellen Perkins wrote, "Without doubt, the number one most psychologically damaging thing you can say to a child is, '*I don't love you*' or '*you were a mistake.*'" It is sad but true that each one of us is responsible for healing the damage that was inflicted on us.

I refer to Louise Hay's book *Heal Your Body* often. In searching for your particular health challenge alphabetically, you will find the probable cause, including an affirmation to create new thought patterns. Louise believed your negative thoughts and what you focus on can create an emotional state which can cause illness. She also believed that positive thoughts and focus could create health. Diagnosed with incurable cervical cancer, Louise concluded that holding on to resentment from childhood abuse and rape contributed to her disease. She also suffered from abuse and domestic violence.

Refusing conventional and medical treatment, she used therapy, forgiveness, reflexology, occasional colonics, and nutrition. She cured her cancer. Later she became an author, teacher, and lecturer, writing and publishing thirty motivational self-help books. Louise is the founder of Hay House Publishing, establishing the First Church of Religious Science. She lived to the ripe old age of ninety.

We talk negatively to ourselves all the time. How about some positive talk? Positive affirmations work on the subconscious part of the brain creating optimism. Optimism creates positive physical and emotional health and requires regular practice for lasting changes. Some psychologists suggest an affirmation should be repeated three to five times a day.

Writing them down and saying them to yourself in a mirror makes them even more effective.

When I read an affirmation that I knew I needed during my recovery time, I wrote it on a post-it note and taped it to my bathroom wall. My family fussed a bit as the wall became plastered with so many. I later removed them and recorded each one on an audiotape. I listened to this forty-five-minute tape every morning for a year as I dressed, bathed, and prepared for my day. I almost had it memorized. I continue to use affirmations and post them on my computer desk.

Some of those personal, powerful affirmations that changed my life were:

I FORGIVE MYSELF AND OTHERS

I LOVE MYSELF JUST THE WAY I AM

I DESERVE LOVE

I NOW CHOOSE TO LET GO OF ALL HURT AND RESENTMENT

I AM THE CREATOR OF MY LIFE

IT'S ONLY A THOUGHT AND A THOUGHT CAN BE CHANGED

I TRUST IN THE PROCESS OF LIFE

IT IS SAFE TO LOOK WITHIN

ALL IS WELL IN MY WORLD

I LOVE CHEF SALADS

These positive affirmations changed my life by building self-confidence. I developed self-love and self-respect and began to realize I deserved the entire loaf of bread rather than just one slice. Never liking vegetables except for potatoes, I began to crave chef salads and still hunger for them today.

One of the most precious gifts our Creator gave us is our mind. How we feel and act depends on what we *choose* to think about. All emotions and actions are preceded by thought. With this great power, you can become the master of your life. You get to choose whatever you want to think in your world. Perception is not necessarily reality. What part of reality is only an illusion, anyway?

"Reality is merely an illusion albeit a very persistent one." - Albert Einstein

I love to ponder the question," If a tree falls in the forest with no one is around to hear it, does it make a sound?" This raises questions about observation and perception. And so, the answer is yes, *and* no? If we think of the word *sound* to mean a human experience, then there is no sound without ears or a measuring device to record it. But as a physical occurrence, even if no one is around, yes, the falling tree makes a sound.

"Reality doesn't exist until observed. The idea of an objective real world whose smallest parts exist objectively in the same sense as stones or trees exist,

independently of whether or not we observe them is impossible." - Werner Heisenberg

Time is a human concept and an illusion. What you read in the prior sentence is now the past. The words you read next are the future. And so, are we not always in the present moment? Time can make us victims. When emotions and thoughts of past events dictate our lives, we miss the present moment's peacefulness. We have the power to choose.

"Peace of mind is not the absence of conflict from life, but the ability to cope with it." - Mahatma Gandhi

Mindfulness is at the root of Buddhism, Taoism, Yoga, and numerous Native-American traditions. It is being in the present moment with full awareness of our thoughts, feelings, bodily sensations, and the surrounding environment. When practicing mindfulness, our thoughts tune into what we're sensing in the present moment, reducing stress and worry. Mindfulness blurs the line between self and others. "Dance like no one is watching." Savor what you are eating or drinking. Look and see everything that your eyes are viewing. Live consciously. Let emotions flow in and out of you. Sometimes I like to lay on the bed with my eyes closed listening to how many sounds I hear. I usually experience five. The sound of my breathing, my heart beating, a clock ticking, the furnace running, a car passing on the street, or a dog barking in the distance are some of the sounds. At times I can hear a wall shifting in the house or the floor creaking.

Being mindful is not easy. We live in a world of responsibility, distraction, performance, worry, and drama. When trying to do too many things, there is an experience of pressure, resistance, and stress. We start believing that we have no control over our schedule and not enough time. Occasionally practicing mindfulness, we are reminded of the peace that is missing.

"The present moment is the only thing where there is no time. It is the point between past and future. It is always there, and it is the only point we can access in time. Everything that happens is happening in the present moment. Everything that ever happened and will ever happen can only happen in the present moment. It is impossible for anything to exist outside of it." - Myrko Thum

I deserve love.

I am good enough.

I am healthy.

I forgive others.

CHAPTER 8

UNCONDITIONAL LOVE
AND ACCEPTANCE

"Life is a Gentle Teacher. She wants to help us learn. The lessons she wants to teach us are the ones we need to learn. We strain and strain, but she will keep repeating the lesson until we learn."
- Immanuel

Unconditional love is love without conditions. It is the type of love existing between a parent and child or a dog and his master. It is a love that is given without expecting love in return, offering love without strings attached. Love with boundaries, however, is necessary. Letting others know where you stand and how you wish to be treated is imperative. If you ignore the need for boundaries, you are offering codependent love. Excusing someone's behavior for the sake of love is not healthy.

Love connects us to our true nature. We can open to love by not judging, complaining, or finding fault in ourselves and others. Be compassionate with yourself. Life is not easy.

People who possess empathy, inspire action, and social change challenge prejudice. They tend to be good listeners striking up conversations with strangers.

Many put into practice the Native American proverb, "Walk a mile in another man's moccasins before you criticize him."

When things get tough, I trust that somewhere deep inside of me, there is a strength and courage I must possess to have said *yes* to this adventure. Self-love is not selfish; it is necessary. If every person in the world demonstrated self-love, all would develop a more profound capacity to love one another. Wars would not exist. When you love yourself first, the world will love you back.

"How can you feel the love of God if you do not love yourself? Are they not one and the same thing?" - Ram Dass, *IMMANUEL'S BOOK*

John Lennon knew it. As an extremist, he is one of the most influential people in history. John's message of peace, love, and happiness will forever be remembered. The media in the sixties and seventies viewed him as cynical, viewing him as a threat. False claims were made about his real personality. John Lennon was one of the infamous Beatles, a peaceful man, and a musical pioneer introducing the world to rock and roll. He wrote numerous peace and politics songs, including *Imagine*, *Give Peace a Chance,* and *Power to the People.* I am a dreamer, as was John Lennon, dreaming that the world could be as *One.*

At mom's life celebration, I asked Lisa to sing *Imagine* as a message for family unity and peace. The lyrics in this song are about believing in the possibilities of hope, freedom, and peace to create a better human existence in our world.

"Peace is the result of retraining your mind to process life as it is, rather than as you think it should be." - Wayne W. Dyer

A few years ago, I heard about *The Christmas Truce of 1914*. World War I ravaged a continent, leaving destruction behind with millions of deaths. The Western Front was a term used to describe the contested armed frontier between lands controlled by Germany to the east and the Allies to the west. The western front called for a truce from Christmas Eve through Christmas Day.

Sounds of exploding shells and gunfire faded as evening approached. Christmas carols filled the silence, and soldiers were coming out of their trenches exchanging gifts of rations and cigarettes. Just hours earlier, those who were exchanging gunfire were now passing around family photos and playing soccer. This remarkable, peaceful day was also called *the Miracle on the Western Front.*

"How marvelously wonderful, yet how strange it was. Thus Christmas, a celebration of love, managed to bring mortal enemies together as friends for a time," recalled German Lieutenant Kurt Zehmisch. Of course, this did not last, the soldiers went back into the trenches, and World Was I carried on for decades.

Can you imagine the feelings and emotions these soldiers felt before and after this brief truce? I wonder what went through their minds as they resumed their combat roles engaging in fighting the enemy? Did I kill the soldier whose family I saw photos of or played soccer with?"

Unfortunately, some reasons that peace is absent from some parts of the world are due to racial prejudice or hatred built based on social class, color, creed, or sex. In international relations, peace is nonexistent among nations, attributed to differences in their economic or political systems. Discrimination affects people's opportunities, their well-being, as well as their sense of potential. Relentless exposure to discrimination can lead individuals to internalize the prejudice or stigma directed against them, manifesting in shame, low self-esteem, fear and stress, and poor health.

Once I read, "There is no right or wrong, good or bad, black or white, day or night." Wow, I can finally let go of guilt and judgment. I felt like one hundred pounds had fallen from my shoulders. I realized the earth is a school where you have opportunities to grow and learn. We are souls having a human experience. I now choose to use the word *lesson* instead of *mistake* or *sin.* This word choice benefits me in accepting myself and others unconditionally.

Being receptive to a wide variety of ideas, arguments, and information is open-mindedness. With extreme division in the world today, it is more important than ever to step outside our comfort zones considering others' viewpoints and perceptions. Life is an ongoing learning process. There are always further discoveries that we can make about ourselves and the world. The world is constantly evolving.

It is estimated that one in ten adults suffers from some type of mood disorder. Mood swings are expected from time to time, but those with mood disorders live with more unrelieved, constant, and severe symptoms disrupting their daily lives. The most common mood disorders are major depression, bipolar disorder, substance-induced mood disorder, and dysthymia (chronic depression). Feelings like persistent sadness, anxiety, emptiness, hopelessness, low self-esteem, excessive guilt, and decreased energy, accompany these disorders. Antidepressants, psychotherapy, and self-care can help. Researchers are studying the association between foods and the brain with ten nutrients that can combat depression and boost moods, such as calcium, chromium, folate, iron, magnesium, omega-3 fatty acids, vitamins B6, B11, D, and zinc.

I am sympathetic to those who choose suicide and may have to return for the same lesson. Suicide is tragic as well as mysterious, leaving loved ones behind with tremendous guilt. While there are no clear warning signs, many factors lead a person to decide to take their own life. Depression, mental illness, childhood sexual abuse, rape, physical abuse, chronic pain, and family histories of suicide all play a role. A person with chronic pain or a terminal illness fears losing their independence, feeling hopeless, and doesn't want to be a burden to others. With deep feelings of hopelessness, ending your own life seems to be the only solution. Being under the influence of drugs and alcohol can make people with problems act more impulsively, choosing suicide.

The depths of depression (when you have to reach up to touch the bottom) are something you never want to experience. If you ever experienced it, you never want to go there again. The feeling is indescribable, and I thank God we forget the intensity of it. Depression is genetic, involving the chemical imbalance of serotonin as a significant factor. Antidepressants can replace serotonin, reducing pain and anxiety. Seeking help for depression is no different than seeing a doctor for a broken leg. A lack of serotonin is simply a lack of a chemical that is typically produced in the brain that requires replenishing. Aging reduces the production of the chemical. There is no need for embarrassment. When others say, "*Just shake it off,*" or "Get *over it,*" I cringe.

Having a *dark night of the soul* is different than depression as it is a spiritual form of crisis. However, the symptoms are similar. With feelings of hopelessness, despair, and restlessness, we discover that no one can save us but ourselves making us feel more alone and confused. This dark night of the soul foreshadows deep-seated changes within us, known as spiritual transformation.

"It is the friction within us that causes the mirror of our souls to be polished enough for us to glimpse our True Nature." - Nancy Chalmers, *Ascension: The Dark Night of the Soul*

History repeats itself until the lessons that we need to learn changes our path. Trust me; the opportunity to learn a lesson will appear and reappear until the lesson is learned. Then you'll receive a new lesson. When I realize this is unfolding for me, I grit my teeth, force a smile, and say, "Thank you, God, for more opportunities to learn and grow."

Life is unpredictable as everything changes. Accepting and embracing life can be very difficult as we want to control it whenever possible. In Deepak

Chopra's book *The Seven Laws of Spiritual Success,* the author reveals how to accept what happens to us gracefully. Fighting, resisting, and trying to control use precious energy that can be spent elsewhere and used positively.

Addicts can lose their jobs, health, or their family remaining ignorant of the reason. Substance abuse clouds the mind of the addict. They believe they have complete control, are not harming anyone but themselves, seeing themselves as victims. Some believe they have no power to change and simply do not care what happens to them.

You can avoid reality, but you cannot avoid the consequences of reality. Those who seek power have an inner need to overcome a feeling of powerlessness, possessing a very competitive nature. Without their power and control, they feel inadequate, unloved, and worthless.

Wherever you go, there you are. If we want to grow spiritually, we must refashion ourselves and not the people, places, or things around us. All we are given is ourselves. That is the only thing we have control over. When we change who and what are within our hearts, our lives follow suit, changing too.

The first step in the twelve-step program is, "We admitted we were powerless over alcohol and that our lives had become unmanageable." Admitting powerlessness puts you in a position of humility and receptivity. Asking for help and support from people who love and care about you is essential for success. No matter what you have done, many will still love you. That is unconditional love.

The ultimate and most difficult lesson for all of us is to learn unconditional love and acceptance for ourselves and others. How can we love a new baby so unconditionally and find it extremely hard to love ourselves? I believe this is one of the hardest life lessons. The critical self can be cruel and judgmental. We look in the mirror, viewing ourselves as too fat, too thin, too tall, or too short. "I am not educated enough. I am not rich enough. Who would want to be with me looking like this?" We are continually striving for perfection.

Mistakes are not failures. I prefer to call them lessons. When shifting this thinking, we will not be so hard on ourselves, as well as others. Accept the fact that something we *did* is separate from *who we are* and who we are trying to be. The road to redemption starts with the understanding that we can transcend this by forgiving ourselves and by using self-compassion.

Think about a mistake you've made recently. Everyone has with their kids, partners, coworkers, and friends. Pick one and think about the narrative you told yourself in the outcome. Now discard that feeling of guilt and throw it in the trash. You don't need it anymore. Find a mirror and admit to yourself that you are learning a lesson in this earth school called *life* and are progressing to a new level/grade. Contact the person you hurt, owning up to your mistake. Or send them a text or email with an apology. The more we do this, the more authentic, and rewarding our relationships will be, which is an excellent example for others.

Heart is an international peer-reviewed journal that keeps cardiologists up to date with relevant research advances in cardiovascular disease. The new study revealed last week that daytime naps once or twice a week may reduce the risk of heart attacks, strokes, and heart failure by half. The Spanish Society of Primary Care Physicians has been declaring this for years, asserting that naps also improve memory and alertness.

My suggestions for a healthier, happier society are taking daily naps and working four-day workweeks. Stress levels, heart attacks, and individual happiness would affect our world in a very positive way.

"The human is the only animal on earth that pays a thousand times for the same mistake. The rest of the animals pay once for every mistake they make. But not us. We make a mistake, we judge ourselves, we find ourselves guilty, and we punish ourselves. If justice exists, then that was enough. We don't need to do it again. But every time we remember, we judge ourselves again, we are guilty again, and we punish ourselves again, and again, and again." - Don Miguel Ruiz, *The Four Agreements*

We say that we love ourselves, but do we care about ourselves as much as we do others? That is not selfish; it is self-love. When you love and accept yourself, you will develop healthy and happy relationships with others. Treat yourself as you would your children or friends. Ask what is important to you, setting boundaries for yourself. Your feelings tell you when someone has hurt you. Let others know what you will and will not tolerate. Being assertive and taking actions to get your own needs met will build your self-esteem. You will show yourself and others that you deserve to be loved and cherished.

Discover who you are and what your purpose is in this lifetime. Do the things that make you happy and fulfilled. You don't need other peoples' permission to do the things that you love. This is your life, and you are in charge of your happiness. The better you feel, the more you can be there for others. Realize that you are worthy and deserving of love. You are one of a kind, and there will never be anyone like you again. You were made in the image and likeness of God/Universe, your creator. Perceiving yourself in any other respect is the judgment of your Maker. God does not make junk. That doesn't mean there is no room to grow and learn as that is the nature of this adventure called life. Learning to love yourself *is* the greatest love of all and begins with acceptance.

Inner child work allowed me to view myself as a sweet, innocent little girl needing love and attention. This permitted me to feel compassion for myself as I learned how to parent her. Mary Marcia can be fun and feisty, but inappropriate at times. When I need only my adult self to be present, I will instruct her to take a nap. Even though she *is* me, it is easier to love, accept, and feel compassion for the little me.

I try to remember to do something nice for myself each day, like preparing a coffee mocha after work while watching *Let's Make a Deal*. Or by purchasing a new blouse, not because I need it, but because it is beautiful. Occasionally I will splurge on lunch rather than stopping home for a sandwich. Wear that new dress or pair of shoes you are saving for special occasions. This is your life right here and now. Love who you are and treat yourself as you would your precious child or grandchild.

"When you begin to blossom and glow and dance down the street just because you are happy and you know the illusion is your creation here for your own education, and you can alter it anytime you want simply by the act of self-love, then you are free. You are preparing your pathway Home whenever you are ready to come." – Ram Dass, *Immanuel's Book*

How powerful these words are and how liberating! I am a co-creator with God. I am the captain of my ship!

All of us are a part of the Whole. I visualize God/Universe as a giant mirror broken into millions of pieces. Each little bit makes up the whole. Fragments can be small, large, black, white, shiny, sharp, or dull. Each of us is a piece of that sizable broken mirror embodied as God. When open-hearted and clear-minded, we are inclined to love every human being for all of who they are. Their struggles, successes, joys, and pains, belong to us as well.

Namaste is an ancient Sanskrit greeting still used every day in India. The saying in Hindi translates to:

"I honor the place in you where Spirit lives.
I honor the place in you, which is
Of Love, of Truth, of Light, of Peace
When you are in that place in you
And I am in that place in me
Then we are One."

I recall a flyer I designed when teaching the Parent Education Nurturing Program. Empowering parents and their children by developing self-love and self-acceptance was a critical aspect. I named the brochure "Dare to be Different - Dare to by You!" It reads as follows:

"I can tell you what the journey is not about. It is not about being whoever you were taught you ought to be. It is not about obeying the histories related by your well-meaning families. It is not about the givens of the world. It is not about conforming to a concept, even such a concept of enlightenment. Your love is not about pleasing someone else. That does not mean you are thoughtless, rude, arrogant, or lacking in compassion. It means that you are who you really are. You have spent this lifetime searching for perfect love. You have looked to teachers, to religion, to books, to ideas, to philosophies, why, even to spirits, and you have not yet found the promise of that perfection because you have been looking outside yourselves. Such a love awaits within you." - Immanuel

CHAPTER 9

ANASTANZA, ANGELS AND HEALING

"Spiritual growth comes from finding the truth
in our individual ways throughout life and
accepting ordination to better serve.
Each of us must find our own Holy Grail."
- Universal Ministries

After enduring the dark, lonely tunnel of transformation and healing, my heart was open to spirituality. I trusted intuition to lead me. Have you ever turned on the radio and heard a song playing that connects you to a loved one just when you were thinking of them? We all experience haunting coincidences. Synchronicity provides us with sudden glimpses of an expanded reality, making us feel like we are characters in a larger, mystical universe. Many people believe that the Universe, angels, or God cause synchronicity. These occurrences can serve to teach us, to stop us, pondering the question, "Is there is something I need to pay attention to here?"

Angels are happy to communicate their presence with us, realizing evidence reinforces our belief in them. I've been nudged numerous times by my angelic guides.

I recall meeting a man with whom I had spent five years. When our eyes first met, something felt familiar, stopping us both in our tracks to talk. The relationship became a friendship, but he wanted to take it further. I made it clear that I did not. One night he asked me over to see his new apartment offering to grill me a steak. Not wanting to hurt his feelings, I obliged, and a steak on the grill sounded good. When we talked on the sofa, I looked into his eyes, and my interest in him suddenly shifted. I call this an "angel nudge." This type of incident has occurred a few times in my life when I suddenly viewed someone differently. After I became aware of his addiction, it impacted our relationship immensely. Giving him the ultimatum to seek help or ending the relationship was my only choice. He chose addiction counseling and treatment with an accomplished recovery. A few years later, we fell out of love and moved on to other relationships, offering us more opportunities to grow. His soul assisted me in gaining confidence, respect, and strength in myself. From the beginning, intuition told me that we would be together for five years, which was the extent of our relationship. Our souls advanced as a consequence, and we remain friends, today.

Plenty of Fish was an official dating website where you could view profiles with photos of people searching for a hookup, date, or life partner. A lesson I learned quickly was that physical attraction is necessary. When scanning profiles, if a photo was not attached, I quickly skipped to the next. One evening I saw a profile without a photo but was moved to read it. This man stated that he had all of his body parts. I thought to myself," Who on earth would say something like that when introducing himself on a profile?" I had to find out. Being a curious individual, I messaged this interesting fellow, and we have been together for fifteen years. I recall two other male friendships suddenly changing to love. Both were highly instrumental in my growth.

An angel prompted me to begin to write my first book after hearing a particular comment from my dentist. Her statement," That could be a chapter in your book" prompted me to start the book the following morning. My fingers typed for hours. It brings me great comfort knowing angel guides are supporting my highest good.

A clairvoyant disclosed her vision of my guardian angel. She noted angels have no gender, but this angel resembled a seven-foot male stating his name was Anastanza. "When you cry, Anastanza folds his wings around you, enveloping you with comfort," she described. I apply this visualization as needed: talking to Anastanza, my Reiki guides, and all angel guides every day.

Angels can bring you messages through music and lyrics. One morning, while bathing, with my head submerged in a tub of water, I asked Anastanza to please give me a sign that he was present. When emerging from under the water, Celine Dion was singing *I'm Your Angel* on the radio. I cried tears of joy, giving thanks for this divine revelation. It doesn't get any more obvious than this!

Angels have intervened in my life, rescuing me on several occasions. With only fingers clutching to the side of a door frame, angels tightly secured my body when my intoxicated ex was attempting to push me down a flight of basement stairs. This man possessed the strength of a bull, and there was no other way I could stay in place. On another occasion, I was driving over a hill coming upon a stopped car. It happened so suddenly that there was no time to react. It felt like someone had taken over the steering wheel with me as I swerved around the stopped vehicle, onto the grass, and back onto the road. I do not doubt that an angel had taken control of the truck, saving us from an inevitable collision. I am also convinced that my guardian angel removed the painful memory of an enraged brother choking me. Psychologists call it dissociative amnesia when a person blocks out certain information associated with a traumatic event.

Such scenarios are commonly reported by people who believe that their guardian angels are protecting them. Guardian angels may protect you from harm, either by rescuing you from danger or by preventing you from entering a dangerous situation.

Anastanza is my bodyguard who will always be with me. He protects me from danger, keeping me safe. My angel offers moral guidance, helps me become a stronger person guiding me to accomplish my soul purpose in this lifetime. I love to hear people tell angel stories and read about how angels have interceded in their lives. We would all feel a little more secure if we realized the constant presence of loving angels surrounding us. I believe we each have a special Guardian Angel and several other angel guides that watch over us.

Our angels are working to help us, but sometimes we are too occupied with our thoughts, desires, worries, or concerns to pay close enough attention to them. Create a quiet and peaceful time to call upon your angels for help, being quietly receptive to their answers. We only need to remember to ask for their help verbally through our thoughts. I utilize the Healing with the Angels card deck to get answers to my questions. Your angels know your thoughts and feelings, love you unconditionally, focusing exclusively on helping you grow, prosper, and evolve in this lifetime. You are their sole purpose and occupation, and they understand your every need. Trust them to guide you to your highest good in every situation. Your relationship with them will become closer and more intimate, helping you understand the Divine Order that is in everything around you.

The first time I saw the movie *The Green Mile*, an awakening with intense desire came over me as I viewed the inmate healing the warden's wife. It is written that if you were attuned to Reiki in a previous lifetime, you would be drawn to it again. Soon after, I attended an introductory class to Reiki, locating a master/teacher. Within two years, I received all three attunements certifying me as a Reiki/Seichim Master.

Each attunement's energy works with you on a different level. The first attunement affected my emotional level. I cried uncontrollably with joy as something was released in me, filling me with *Ki* energy.

Eager to give the gift of reiki energy, Mom agreed to be my first client. The massage table had not arrived, so I asked her to lay on her dining room table, making her comfortable with lots of pillows. I played a meditation CD, lit candles, recited a prayer, drew the Cho Ku Rei symbol on her body with my hands, and began. I had to do this by the book. I remember the love I felt for her when delivering reiki to her heart chakra. There were tears in my eyes as the connection was something I always desired. I expressed how much love I was feeling for her. I told her someday in another lifetime I would like to be her mother. She replied, "That would be great!"

After the second attunement, I was confronted with numerous eye surgeries. The energy was affecting my physical level. What was I not seeing, or what did I need to see metaphysically?

The third attunement included Seichim energy. Seichim/Sekhem is a form of Universal energy that was used for healing in Ancient Egypt. This energy focuses on the heart center healing on all levels. Seichim operates on a higher vibration than Reiki and is much needed in our world today. I sensed this angelic realm for two glorious weeks experiencing total peace and joy within. I hoped it would last indefinitely, but my little ego crept back into my world.

"The Reiki attunement is a powerful spiritual experience. The attunement energies are channeled into the student through the Reiki Master. The process is guided by the Rei or God-consciousness and makes adjustments in the process depending on the needs of each student. The attunement is also attended by Reiki guides and other spiritual beings who help implement the process. Many report having mystical experiences involving personal messages, healings, visions, and past life experiences." - Family of Light Holistic Center

I moved to another state visiting mom every other weekend, giving her Reiki. The gift of touch is very therapeutic, especially for the elderly and those who live alone. Mom habitually said, *"Your hands are incredibly hot."* I always replied, "That's the reiki, mom. You need it here."

One specific treatment I will never forget, recalling the moment often. With mom lying back in the recliner, I could sit on a chair behind her, starting the treatment with the head positions. Reiki on the brain is amazing. Later, as I moved my hands to the heart chakra, she grasped them, expressing how much she loved me. She said," I love you so much. I love you the most." Even now, this brings tears to my eyes. I realized how much I meant to her. Her hands were as soft as rose petals, as I can still feel them. We both progressed profoundly together in our journey to find love. What a gift I was given!

I was summoned to devote my life to be of service to humanity. I accepted this call, vowing to serve humanity, spreading love into the world as an ordained minister. I wanted to join the (SHES) International Assembly of Spiritual Healers and Earth Stewards ministry, so my Reiki teacher could also ordain me, but she moved to Sedona, Arizona, soon after. After searching, I found Universal Ministries, sent in the form with an essay on my background with reasons I desired to be ordained. I realized it was the vow that mattered the most. The Doctrine of Universal Ministries states, "Do what is right, live fruitful lives, be true to ourselves and the God each of us worship, while causing no harm to others, and accept the individual's right to worship as they see fit within the laws of their respected countries."

Revelations with visions were occurring between my dream state and consciousness. Once, I viewed huge boulders shaped into the word *TRUST* in capital letters. Not long after this, my daughter gifted me with a card containing my name with its meaning. It read: "Mary – Trust in the Lord with all your heart and lean not on your own understanding." Another time in that same state, I felt the love that Lisa had for her daughter. Once on a daily walk, I asked for a sign from my guides. I walked around a corner, joyfully discovering a sidewalk and lawn filled with hundreds of beautiful white feathers. Feathers are incredibly significant for angelic communication. White small feathers found together indicate your guardian angel, and many angels are around you.

There are similarities in the healings of Jesus and Reiki. Many miracles were accomplished by the laying on of hands. Another correlation is the fact that Jesus could pass the power to heal on to others, which is similar to the Reiki attunement process. It is not known what that power was, but passing it on is similar to reiki's transfer.

"I tell you the truth; anyone who has faith in me can do the same miracles I have done and even greater than these you will do." - John 14:11

"What about faith? While faith was required for many of the healings he performed, it appears that the healing Jesus did with his hands did not require faith. Mark 6:5-6 *states," He could not do any miracles there,*

except lay his hands on a few sick people and heal them. He was amazed at their lack of faith." And so, even though they did not believe, Jesus was still able to use the laying of hands to heal. This is one of the crucial aspects of Reiki. It does not require faith on the part of those receiving treatment for the Reiki to work."
- William Lee Rand, *International Center for Reiki*

Dis-ease is an abnormal condition in our bodies. Experiencing a healthy body is having a natural flow of *Ki* or *Chi* energy. Universal life force energy is in every living thing. Listen and trust your body's communication. When your body needs rest, you will feel tired. Do not feel guilty for sleeping or taking naps. That is self-love and self-care, respecting the Creator who made you. In that higher frequency of love, healing can occur. Trust your intuition as to what you need. Prayer is you talking to God; intuition is God talking to you.

Chiropractic is a health care profession that focuses on disorders of the musculoskeletal system and the nervous system and how they affect general health. Afflictions include back pain, neck pain, joint pain, headaches, etc. Treatment typically involves spinal manipulation and sometimes, therapy. With chiropractic, I avoided two surgeries for carpal tunnel on both wrists and neck surgery.

A surgeon usually suggests surgery for treatment; a physician may prescribe medication, and a massage therapist will recommend a massage. You get the idea. Exploring alternative medicine and holistic approaches can prevent aggressive procedures and treatments. Once viewed as quackery, chiropractic medicine has come a long way and is covered by most insurance companies. Chiropractors must earn a Doctor of Chiropractic degree and a state license taking four years to complete and require at least three years of undergraduate college education for admission. Parker College states chiropractors spend more than three hundred and seventy more classroom hours than doctors. Chiropractic medicine is certainly worth a try.

Our energy body is a reflection of our consciousness. If you have ever practiced yoga, you've probably heard about the body's four layers: the physical, emotional, mental, and energy body. The energy and physical bodies impact each other. Our consciousness operates better when we have a healthy physical foundation. Chakras are energy vortexes in our bodies. These disks of spinning energy each correspond to specific nerve bundles and major organs. Chakras play an essential role in the flow of energy in your body. The word chakra means *wheel* or *circle* in Sanskrit, dating back to ancient Eastern traditions.

Internal energy is known as *chi, prana,* or *life force energy.* Our chakras interpret sensory information from the outside world around us. Most people have heard of the seven main chakras, which connect to major nerve clusters and endocrine glands at points along the spine. The human body is made of energy. In addition to the 114 chakras, it also has 71,000 energy channels, along which vital energy or prana moves. The use of energy scanning devices such as *CAT* scans, *PET* scans, and *MRIs* relies upon the fact that bio-energetic emissions exist. These readings are possible because diseased tissue gives off a distinctive and uncommon pattern different from healthy cells.

Chakras work as filters from the chaos of the outside world. Physical, mental, or emotional upsets can block a chakra. Life never stops presenting us with challenges. Having your chakras checked is maintenance for your body's energy system. The longer a chakra is closed, blocked, or unbalanced, the more likely you are to develop a severe physical or emotional illness. To function at their best, your chakras need to stay open or balanced. If they get blocked, you may experience physical or emotional symptoms related to a particular chakra.

In my practice, I use the pendulum to check chakras, open them with Reiki and crystals, and recheck them afterward with the pendulum. You will find that there are many ways to open your chakras if you search the internet.

I witnessed miracles with Reiki. You don't always get results after giving a treatment, but with some treatments, I did receive feedback. I call the client a few days later and ask how they are feeling with a reminder to drink more water. A common comment is that they are more relaxed and peaceful. Feedback is educational for the teacher, and explanations are sometimes necessary for the receiver.

Reiki's Universal Life Force energy relieves pain, anxiety, illness, and disease while balancing the person's chakras and aura. It also lowers blood pressure, speeding the healing process as emotional calming occurs. The energy has an intelligence of its own, affecting the body, mind, and spirit, and is focused on where healing is needed most at that time.

A friend in distress called me on a Friday, stating his doctor had arranged an appointment for him with a specialist for the following Monday. A suspicious lesion was discovered in his throat during an exam. Frantic and worried about cancer, he indicated he had smoked heavily for over thirty years. I administered Reiki to him on Sunday. The following day he phoned me after his appointment. Relieved and joyful, he relayed that this doctor could not locate any throat lesions.

A female client contacted me to schedule a Reiki treatment. She sounded distraught and concerned about a uterine tumor a doctor had found. The growth was scheduled to be removed the next week. I administered Reiki the following day. The gynecologist informed her that she might not be able to conceive children. To become a mother was her greatest desire. When the surgeon opened her to remove the growth, she was startled to see the tumor had moved to another area and had shrunk. She checked the ultrasound to be sure she was correct. This lady has since conceived and delivered three healthy children.

I also remember treating a young boy who fell off a slide at a playground, landing on his head. Moaning and holding his head, I immediately thought of a brain concussion. His mother hurried over to him. I asked her if I could touch him. She said, "Yes." I explained Reiki to her as the energy was flowing into his head. Suddenly, after a few minutes, the boy fled my hands and bolted back up the slide as if nothing had happened.

With Reiki, the universal life force energy is transmitted into the crown chakra and through the attuned practitioner's hands. The practitioner is merely a channel for the energy to flow through. Source energy does all the work.

A few years after discovering EFT (Emotional Freedom Technique), I enrolled in an introductory class at a church I attended. I was amazed at the effectiveness of this psychological acupressure technique! I continued to receive numerous certifications online and was thrilled to speak on the phone with founder Gary Craig when ordering CD training sets. Gary Craig says, "Try it on anything and everything!" The only reason a person becomes an EFT practitioner is to be of service in the healing and transformation of people's lives, including their own. EFT (also called psychological acupressure) was developed in the 1990s and has become increasingly popular. Acupuncture is an ancient healing practice of traditional Chinese medicine. Thin needles are inserted into the skin at specific points. Acupuncture is used to relieve pain and many other conditions. Pressure and tapping on these meridian points are also effective.

EFT is based on the concept that all negative emotions disrupt the body's energy system. Pain is an indicator of needed healing, offering a doorway to recovery. This therapeutic psychological tool clears negative emotions healing trauma, PTSD, addictions, phobias, disorders, and physical pain. EFT is a form of acupuncture without needles. Fingertips are used to tap and stimulate specific energy points on the body. By tapping on these points, signals are sent to parts of the brain that control stress and emotion. This energy flows through the body restoring balance to the body's energy system. In restoring this balance, past painful emotions caused by a difficult experience or negative experience are relieved. Disruptions of energy are why we have emotional issues like grief, anger, guilt, depression, trauma, and fear. Both physical and achievement problems often have emotional roots as well. Remember, the natural state of the body is good health and well-being.

Acupuncturists study and use over three hundred meridian points on the body. The EFT technique recognizes the fact that the twelve meridians and two governing vessels interconnect. As a consequence, the energy sent down one pathway influences the other pathways. That is why only a few pathways for successful results are addressed.

To begin, the issue or problem is identified, and the emotion is uncovered. The intensity of the emotion is given a number from 0-10. This is called (SUDS) the Subjective Units of Distress Scale. A phrase is then designed to acknowledge the problem with how you accept yourself despite it. The language used is targeted at the negative. This wording is an essential part of the process because it tells our system what we are working on. This, in turn, creates energy disruptions in your system so the negative can be neutralized with tapping.

While maintaining your mental focus on the issue, fingertips are used to tap five to seven times each on nine of the body's meridian points. While concentrating on accepting and resolving negative emotions, tapping on these points accesses your body's natural energy, restoring it to a balanced state.

After a round of tapping, the emotions' intensity is compared and measured for progress. Remember, when a very traumatic and emotional situation is addressed, this will be the final time you will have to experience the pain associated with the incident. The memory will remain and magically, the emotional pain will disappear.

A certified practitioner is trained to help you explore parts of your past, discovering the root causes of problems. Confidentiality and feeling safe are a must. They see your issue from a different perspective than you, without the feelings and memories. The ability to tune into the problem is the most critical factor for success, and experienced therapists have the training to achieve this. Good practitioners have a success rate of eighty to one hundred percent. They also know extra tapping points with additional techniques to help in complex cases. A practitioner may need another practitioner to help them discover the underlying components of a problem. EFT works like psychotherapy but with tapping. You can learn how to tap on yourself, but sometimes another person tapping on you fills the need for touching and nurturing.

Like puzzle pieces, aspects are smaller parts of an issue. For example, when anger is released, sadness emerges, or another memory and emotion will show up. Addictions are usually multifaceted, containing many individual parts that will require addressing. All aspects need to be resolved for good results, and an EFT practitioner is trained to address this.

Quantum physicists are finding more evidence that we are energy beings vibrating at our own pace. Each one of us radiates with a unique energy signature. If you could observe an atom with a microscope, you would see a small, invisible tornado-like vortex. If the atom is made of invisible energy having no physical structure, we have no physical structure, and neither does anything that appears solid. All of us are composed of pure energy. To me, energy-induced healing modalities make total sense.

When two people resonate with each other, they are on the same synchronized vibration. Have you ever been in conversation with someone you just met, feeling an instant connection? Your energies were vibrating on the same frequency as musical tones and radio waves.

Life is experienced within our consciousness. Quantum physics states that our consciousness' activity affects the behavior of atoms, so our entire being exists in an interactive field of energy. Astrology is also based on energy. Our astrological birth chart is a map of an individual's energy pattern depending on the alignment of the planets at the time of one's birth. Each zodiac sign gives off a different type of energy. Healing in this force field is quite common in Eastern medicine, and the advancement of dual healing has many followers in numerous professions.

EMDR (Eye Movement Desensitization and Reprocessing) therapy is a form of psychotherapy in which a subject will recall traumatic memories while moving their eyes from side to side in a rhythmic pattern. It has an eighty percent effective treatment for PTSD, anxiety, depression, and panic disorders, being very similar to the Emotional Freedom Technique using the Nine Gamut procedure. This treatment has also shown success in decreasing adverse effects associated with PTSD.

Post-Traumatic Stress Disorder is a mental health condition that's triggered by experiencing or witnessing a terrifying event. Symptoms include flashbacks, nightmares, severe anxiety, uncontrollable thoughts, and memories of the episode that are symptomatic. If not treated, symptoms can last for months or years. PTSD can affect anyone who experiences trauma. In writing this book, I realized I suffered this illness due to circumstances when my father died. I also experienced PTSD after a car accident that totaled our pickup and recreational vehicle this spring.

It is far too familiar for military veterans, affecting more than thirty percent who have been in war zones. The nervous system remains stuck, unable to return to its normal state. Veterans can have flashbacks their entire lives, with fireworks being huge triggers.

Evidence demonstrating the effectiveness of EFT has steadily increased in recent years. Studies reveal eighty-four to ninety percent of victims show improvement with person-to-person deliverance of this technique as a highly effective treatment. Tapping on certain energy meridians while emotions are high sends signals to the part of the brain that controls stress and emotion. With trauma, memories remain; however, the emotions attached to them are permanently erased. I find similarity with treating aspects to removing the layers of an onion. Aspects are various details or remnants of an issue. When one has vanished, another may appear to exhibit a different emotion. And so, it continues, especially with the multi-layered complexity of addictions.

Some people state that happiness is a choice, but so is misery. I question this statement as I do not think it's that simple. Everyone has been conditioned in their life, and I know EFT can change that conditioning.

"Our sadness is an energy we discharge in order to heal. Sadness is painful. We try to avoid it. Actually, discharging sadness releases the energy involved in our emotional pain." - John Bradshaw

How we relate to our experiences is what drives our emotions. By containing our emotions, we freeze the pain within us. Placing it on the back burner does not release it. It is always there, affecting us consciously or unconsciously.

As children, we were rewarded when we did well and punished when we did not. We ended up brainwashed by society's rules, afraid of rejection, seeking merit for what we do. This teaches us to judge ourselves whenever we mess up. We tend to personalize our experiences. By don Ruiz Miguel, *The Four Agreements* reveals the source of self-limiting beliefs that rob us of joy, creating needless suffering. Periodically, I need reminders of the second agreement, "Don't Take Anything Personally." Everyone lives in their minds, and their worlds are entirely different than ours. People react from within themselves, and not because of us. We assume they know what is in our world. Every one of us has a different view and a different perception. That is what makes us unique.

This book's insights represent those possessed by the *Toltecs* (now Mexico) a thousand years ago. They are very similar concepts used by modern psychologists. Ruiz says that all children are born perfectly loving, playful, and genuine. However, parents condition their children with standards of behavior and conditions of worth. It is like giving them a life script to live by. Much of this is necessary, but some are illogical and limiting. Children do not know better and agree to which they are programmed. This is the importance of telling a child they are competent rather than dumb, ambitious rather than lazy, and so forth.

The Four Agreements are described in more detail in don Miguel Ruiz's book, but here is a short description of each.

1. BE IMPECCABLE WITH YOUR WORD. Our words create our reality. Rid yourself of negative self-talk and irrational dialogue. To be impeccable with your word is, to tell the truth, saying things that positively influence yourself and others. Be careful with lies, gossip, and making empty promises. When we hurt others, we hurt ourselves.

2. DON'T TAKE ANYTHING PERSONALLY. Every person sees the world differently. To not take anything personally is to acknowledge that when someone gives us feedback about our behavior, it only reflects on them and how they view the world.

3. DON'T MAKE ASSUMPTIONS. None of us can read minds. Assuming that you know what other people are thinking or feeling about you is a limiting thought. We often jump to conclusions based on our thinking.

4. ALWAYS DO YOUR BEST. Pushing yourself too hard causes oversights, frustration, and anxiety. But you cannot achieve goals by being lazy. Put an honest effort into your life, knowing that some days will be more

productive than others. Always do your best. Do not let your inner judge shame you.

Don Miguel Ruiz states, "There is a huge amount of freedom that comes to you when you take nothing personally." I highly recommend this short book full of enormous wisdom and knowledge. I have read it many times.

We have the power to choose our beliefs. Core beliefs shape our reality. If you believe that you do not deserve love, that you are "damaged goods" or that no one loves you, then this is what you will experience in your world. This is also true of how you look at others and society. Believing that "people only care about themselves" or are "out to get you" shapes your reality. Beliefs and attitudes are usually inherited from our family, or we unconsciously internalize them from others. When examining your viewpoints, do they ring true for your personal and unique consciousness? Notice the beliefs you have. Are they based on fear or do they make you happy?

The realization of knowing who you truly are and that you are good enough allows you to stop seeking approval from others. Trust your gut and the little voice in your head. When something does not fit right for me, it feels like sandpaper rubbing against my soul. Socrates, the teacher of Plato, states, "The unexamined life is not a life worth living."

After reading the book *In God's Truth* by Nick Bunick, I was drawn to the number 444, signifying the power of God's love. The number (4) is not only my favorite number, but my mother's (4) and my daughter's (4).

In the book *Angel Numbers* by Doreen Virtue, Ph. D., and Lynette Brown, the number 444 general meaning reads as follows: "Thousands of angels surround you at this moment; loving and supporting you. You have a very strong and clear connection with the angelic realm and are an Earth angel yourself. You have nothing to fear – all is well."

I will wake up at 4:44 am or notice the time at 4:44 pm. I see 444 in phone numbers, in pricing, addresses, digital devices, and license plates. I recite this prayer that I composed when that number appears to me.

"Peace and love to all the earth, dear God. Peace and love to all your people. Peace and love to the north, east, south, and west. Peace and love above me. Peace and love below me. Peace and love to all the earth, dear God. Peace and love to all your people. Amen. Alleluia. And so, it is." - Mary M Betsworth

My youngest grandson loves to say the words," And so it is." I always let him close the prayer when he is with me.

444 is a communication from God with my angel guides reminding me that everything is happening for my highest good. It also indicates they are present and giving me support. When you pay attention, you see synchronicity with numbers, events, signs, billboards, and people. These are the little messages the Universe and your guides are sending you.

As I sat in my car in a parking lot one afternoon, I reflected on a current relationship. Both of us connected spiritually, believed in the same doctrine, with conversations flowing freely. We were very close friends, but I wanted to take this relationship to an intimate level as I was falling in love with him. As I looked up, a car parked in front of me displayed a license plate that read *NSX PF 444.* I took it as my guides were informing me that there would be no sex with this guy. The letters PF are the two beginning letters of his last name. They were right!

Last week in a dream, I saw Jesus sitting on a bench observing my sister. I looked at him, saying, "I love you." It appeared he was reluctant to remove his attention from her as he took a few seconds to look back at me. He then replied, "I love you," setting his gaze back on her. I said, "I know." Two weeks after this dream, my sister lost her first child. I believe he was preparing her with the strength she needed to endure this loss. I woke up after this dream looking at the digitally displayed alarm clock, and it read 3:33 am. For me, the number 33 is significant for Jesus, as he was crucified at age 33.

CHAPTER 10

LIVING LIFE IN LOVE

"In the infinity of life where I am, all is perfect, whole, and complete. I am always Divinely protected and guided. It is safe for me to look within. It is safe for me to look into the past. It is safe for me to enlarge my viewpoint of life. I am far more than my personality – past, present, and future. I now choose to rise above my personality problems to recognize the magnificence of my being. I am totally willing to learn to love myself. All is well in my world. "
- Louise Haye, *You Can Heal Your Life*

Y ou may remember from your childhood the Hans Christian-Anderson fairy tale titled *The Emperor Has No Clothes*. The story centers on two con men who pretended to be tailors, convincing the emperor they could make him a magical suit, the finest in the land. The magic was that this suit would be invisible to those who were too stupid for their jobs. In fact, the emperor's new suit of clothes was his *birthday suit.*

However, when the emperor paraded in front of his subjects, no one wanted to call out that he had no clothing on. Why? They feared looking stupid. It was only a young child who felt free to speak his mind shouting, "He has no clothes!" The tailors preyed on the emperor's vanity and the fact that people around him wouldn't have the courage to speak up in fear of looking stupid.

Many people are not using their voices to make things better in our world right now. They are expressing their opinions to simply hurt others, shutting out opposing thoughts. The hatred that is seen daily on social media and in the news among politicians and rioters does us no good as a society.

"Never be afraid to raise your voice for honesty and truth and compassion against injustice and lying and greed. If people all over the world would do this, it would change the earth." - William Faulkner

Hatred is learned as we are born to love. Some hearts have become completely closed. They reject those who think or look differently. People who hate are lonely with low self-esteem, are highly insecure, seeking stronger bonds and connections with others who hate.

No one wins in the war of hate, but everyone wins in the name of love. If someone is passionate and committed to attacking you and your viewpoints, don't get caught up in their web of negativity. It takes two sides to start a war. When someone attacks you, avoid getting into a useless battle by avoiding and ignoring them. They will soon stop bothering you as haters love to be hated back, as they will quickly find another enemy that likes to play their game.

Sadly, politics has gradually evolved to become equivalent to religion or supporting a sports team where we hold hands cheering with like-minded people. We get fixated on defending our beliefs as being right or wrong. We disregard other viewpoints caring less and less about understanding the issues. We have to remember that we are supporting a cause, not an individual. Even our worst critics and most stubborn opponents deserve the dignity we wish for ourselves.

Research indicates that hate spreads quicker if it is directed at a group. It fosters a sense of connection that fills a void in a helpless, inadequate, and powerless person. It is a distraction from repressed pain and a temporary distraction from inner suffering. People follow a crowd, especially in public, because everyone wants to be liked and accepted and has a desire to fit in. *"Birds of a feather flock together."*

Society needs individuals more than ever before who are willing to challenge and ask questions - those who will not blindly follow what everyone else is doing. Remaining silent may result in poor decisions being made and affect the future of our world.

"The decisions that you make and the actions that you take upon the earth are the means by which you evolve. These choices affect your evolutionary process. This is so for each person. You can choose to evolve consciously or unconsciously. Your decision to evolve consciously through responsible choice contributes not only to your own evolution but also to the evolution of all those aspects of humanity in which you participate. It is not just you that is evolving

through your decisions, but the entirety of humanity." -
Gary Zukav, *SEAT OF THE SOUL*

There are times when it's necessary to speak up.
It is not about being difficult or making waves. It's
about making sure that all sides of an issue are
considered. It's being curious about what could be,
rather than merely accepting what we are being told.

As a seeker of truth, several relationships ended
when I finally spoke my truth. But by doing so
empowered me personally. If you want to make
changes, be courageous and be prepared to say," The
emperor has no clothes!"

TWO WOLVES - A CHEROKEE PARABLE

"A grandfather is talking with his grandson
and he says there are two wolves inside of us
which are always at battle.
One is a good wolf which represents things
like kindness, bravery, and love.
The other is a bad wolf, which represents
things like greed, hatred, and fear.
The grandson stops and thinks about it
for a second, then he looks up at his
grandfather and says,
"Grandfather, which one wins?"
The grandfather quietly replies,
"The one you feed."

You can have whatever you want in your world.
This is your life and your creation. Feed the good wolf
by spreading kindness, care, and love. Attempt to

understand and forgive those who have not yet learned. Remember, we are in a classroom called Earth. Some souls are in second grade, and some are in seventh. It is unfair to expect a second grader to understand algebra. Everyone is exactly where they are supposed to be, but each always has the opportunity to learn and advance to the next level. Made in the image and likeness of God, everyone has good in them. Choosing what you focus on in others makes your world and your life more pleasant and positive. You give value to others when being in service to them. With time, you get what you give.

Acceptance is a choice with a willingness to tolerate a difficult situation. The important part to focus on is that acceptance is a willful act. The ability to make choices is what makes us humans so incredible. Everyone can exercise free will with the choices we make in life, the paths we go down, and their consequences.

"There are two ways out of a problem: accept what is happening and see the positive, choosing a peaceful state of mind or fight against it and be miserable, struggling against the Universe." - The Tiny Buddha

Many say that even in the afterlife, there is an opportunity for growth. Having father issues, I visited a psychic medium who accelerated my healing process, informing me that my father was present, wanting to tell me that he was sorry. I sobbed like a baby releasing significant inner pain. This event was overwhelmingly powerful as well as healing for us both. She stated she could feel him shift to another level explaining there are opportunities for growth in his dimension, similar to our twelve-step program on earth. I unexpectedly felt his presence in my car the next week and talked to him, even though he had passed over thirty years earlier.

In writing *My Journey Finding Love*, I understood at a deeper level how the trauma of my father's death affected my life in so many ways. I developed a clearer understanding of my inherited woundedness. Soulful connections prompted a deeper inspection and additional healing from past relationships surfaced for healing. The ability to recognize and seize the opportunity for more healing and understanding has indeed been a gift. With a greater ability to see the many blessings in this life, I feel so grateful. All life lessons have a common denominator, and that is love. Feeling love for yourself and others with the same love.

Gratitude works! It creates optimism. It shifts you to a higher frequency, attracting more and more. Each day for a year, I listed three things I was grateful for in a gratitude journal. I could not duplicate entries. It was easy for the first few weeks, and then I needed to search deeper. This daily task supported me in staying positive while discovering the little things in life I appreciate, like a flower, a blade of grass, dandelions, mountains, pizza, and the magnificence of a tree. Being grateful makes you happier. When you choose to appreciate what you have, you intensify your positive emotions, blossoming into a more optimistic and giving person.

"It's a funny thing about life. Once you begin to take note of the things you are grateful for, you begin to lose sight of the things that you lack. " - Germany Kent

I love trees as they are like people. Some are tall, short, slender, stocky, with various colors and stature. They are all beautiful, precisely the way they are. Trees are the biggest plants and are globally vital to our planet. Trees remove harmful gases like carbon dioxide and give off oxygen to help us breathe. They offer food and protection, providing homes for many birds and animals. Timber supplies us with materials for tools and shelters. However, as a native American proverb states, "No tree has branches so foolish as to fight among themselves."

Smiles are contagious. It is very difficult for me not to return a smile. That is another factor I missed during the pandemic. Masks covered smiles. The feel-good neurotransmitters dopamine, endorphins, and serotonin are all released when you smile, relaxing your body and lowering blood pressure. Endorphins also act as a pain reliever. Serotonin serves as an antidepressant. When you smile, you are viewed as better looking, reliable, relaxed, and sincere. People who smile have more positive emotions, stable marriages, increased life spans, with better interpersonal skills than people with negative emotions. The world is simply a better place when people smile, and it is so easy to do.

Working with the DD (Developmental Disability) community has been an impressive learning experience for me. Demonstrations of unconditional love with the "keep life simple" approach have considerably influenced my perception of life. Ninety percent of what we worry about does not happen. I wonder if some souls choose a developmental disability to tolerate another existence on earth, as the insanity and complexity of life can be difficult.

Life is pretty simple. Like nature, we grow from seed, blossom, fade, and then die. It is we humans that make life complicated by overthinking and making mountains out of molehills.

I love the book *Don't Sweat the Small Stuff (and it's all small stuff)* by Richard Carlson, Ph.D. Overthinking and letting the small things in life bother us can drive us crazy. We worry about what people will think if we wear something that is not in style or do not choose to wear a bra or makeup. What will others say about us if we sleep until noon? Being free from judgment, criticism, and fear of what others may think is your true authentic self. This is your life and no one else's. You are only here once in this particular body and lifetime.

Mark Twain's quote says it perfectly. "Work like you don't need the money. Dance like no one is watching, and love like you've never been hurt."

Trust Divine Intelligence and the process of life. Everything works out one way or the other. If it doesn't look like what you expect, trust that it is in your best interest. Everything is happening for your highest good because God loves you.

I believe disasters occur to bring us back to our center of love. Donations generously flow in to support victims. Churches, schools, and businesses open their doors to families for shelter with the realization that we are all One. I read about a new furniture store opening its doors to families for shelter after a hurricane. What a demonstration of love and kindness! Disasters can strengthen a community, giving us a deeper appreciation for nature and each other.

Maslow's original hierarchy begins with the most fundamental impulses (eating, sleeping, excreting) following self-actualization (growing to achieve one's fullest potential). Maslow later added a new layer to the hierarchy, which he called self-transcendence. He concludes that we find actualization by giving ourselves to some higher goal outside the self, such as charitableness and spirituality. This concept of transcendence symbolizes ancient religious and spiritual sources to "find yourself by losing yourself."

"The best way to find yourself is to lose yourself in the service of others." - Mahatma Gandhi

Racism is the belief that some races are better than others Racial discrimination refers to prejudice against individuals because of their skin color, racial or ethnic origin. According to the Webster dictionary, the word "prejudice is a preconceived opinion that is not based on reason or experience." We also see prejudices toward a group based on sex, religion, gender, language, disabilities, appearance, or social status in society. Our brains are designed to categorize. It is essential to know what kind of mushrooms are okay to eat and which ones will make you sick. When we see a tall person, we may think, "They would be a good basketball player." We may believe that African Americans are good dancers, or assume that the elderly walk slower and forget easily. Categorizing can make you prejudiced as well.

As tribal creatures, we are either *for* or *against* and we divide ourselves into groups. Prejudice often has unintended outcomes. But if we think in terms of Oneness, this manner of thinking can be changed. Young children do not see or care about differences. They are usually accepting of one another. Values and attitudes are learned through association, conditioning, and modeling from the world around them. They may associate ethnic groups with crime, poverty, or violence, especially if people laugh at such impolite jokes. The solution is to remind ourselves that not every person is the same. But no matter what issue you bring to the table, whether it be access to health care, immigration, incarceration, the death penalty, marijuana, educational discrepancy, fair living wages, justice for women, pro-life, poverty, or LGBTQ issues are all entangled with and enmeshed in racism.

I could never comprehend this manner of thought. What is the difference if someone is born with black, white, brown, or red skin? Why does it matter if someone has blue, green, brown, or red eyes? I see many colors of hair nowadays like purple, green, pink, and red. As I stated earlier, *"God does not make junk."* Insulting another human being is insulting God, our Creator. People with prejudicial attitudes tend to view everyone who fits into a particular group as being all similar instead of looking at each person as a unique individual. Everyone is born with a soul made unto the image and likeness of God. Each broken splinter in the mirror is a part of God and a part of the Whole.

I do not understand the LBGTQ community, but who am I to judge? As long as they emanate love, what happens in the bedroom is none of my business.

I have met some of the most loving individuals who are gay and occasionally wonder if their souls are higher evolved spiritually. In being discredited and dishonored, prejudice and discrimination create a hostile and stressful social environment that causes many to deal with mental health problems, especially if they attempt to conceal or deny their sexual orientation. This can have serious adverse effects on health and well-being.

Racism is a sickness of the soul. Every person is equal, and unity is a necessity. We are called the United States of America. Even in politics, I sometimes wonder where the *united* is. The division between Democrats and Republicans is not unity. We are souls having a human experience collectively. We have all chosen to exist simultaneously in this same place, to learn and grow together.

Our journey aims to discover wholeness, find our true selves, and the love that lies within us. You can only see the light and goodness in others when you first discover it within yourself. Fear and judgment are dramas of human making, and you can choose to participate in it or not. The drama will continue with or without you.

If the news bothers you, don't listen to it. Instead of feeling hopeless, helpless, and allowing yourself to become angry with what you see happening around the world, you can choose to *"Be that change you wish to see."* - Mahatma Gandhi.

And so, what is the meaning of life? It is love. Love is the life force that connects all things that exist. Love is the glue that holds the universe together. Life is a series of choices, decisions, actions, and inactions.

Our purpose is to grow and evolve, developing mindfulness as we share our experiences with other living souls. A successful life's cornerstone is to have an open mind, an open heart, and to self-manage, your thoughts, feelings, and actions. Shifting from fear to love is a conscious decision to bring out the best in yourself and others in each moment. The greatest gift we can give to ourselves and our children is to willingly transform hurtful patterns which allow us to remain calm while we are faced with opposition.

The *Seven Powers for Conscious Adults* help us self-regulate, become present, conscious, attuned, and responsive to ourselves and our children's needs. Taken from *The Conscious Disciple,* they are as follows:

POWER OF UNITY - We are all in this together.

POWER OF LOVE - Choose to see the best in others.

POWER OF FREE WILL - The only person you can change is you.

POWER OF ATTENTION - Whatever we focus on, we get more of.

POWER OF INTENTION - Mistakes are opportunities to learn.

POWER OF PERCEPTION - No one can make you angry without your permission.

POWER OF ACCEPTANCE - The moment is as it is.

Born in the week of the teacher, I am driven to share my life-learned wisdom with others. The only way out of pain is through it. EFT (Emotional Freedom Technique) could have accelerated my healing process, but I did not become aware of it until later. As a certified practitioner, I use it on myself and others often. It works! You have nothing to lose if you try it. Actually, you do! You can lose all the shame, blame, anger, and guilt you have been hanging on to all these years and later fill that void with love, peace, and compassion for yourself and others.

The answers to finding your authentic self are within you. Be honest with your discontent and find the source. No one has had the perfect childhood, has walked in your shoes, or can understand your life but you. However, if there is something that you got that you did not want or need, or needed something you did not get and it bothers you, then be brave and willing to explore it. It does not make you ungrateful if you choose to dig deeper. Realizing something is missing in your life while maintaining your old views and patterns is not a fun place to be. By choosing to grow and evolve, you will be on a happier, more functional path. There is no need to blame anyone or hold any person accountable. You are not a victim. You alone have the responsibility and power to change. Seek healing by confronting uncomfortable emotions to release them. You will be so happy you chose this route.

Am I there yet? Heck, no. But I have come a long way in gaining some helpful tools and insight, allowing myself a better outlook when things don't go my way. Most times, it is a process I need to go through again and again. It is helpful to realize if it is the adult me or my inner child who is reacting. I don't believe we are finished until we take that final breath and return *Home.*

There will always be disappointments and challenges in life. I tell my grandchildren, "They call this life" when they cannot have what they want. But life also contains joy and pleasure. How else would we know the other if we had not experienced both?

When change occurs, our typical ways of being with old patterns and routines are disturbed. Change is synonymous with life and growth. The challenge is the ability to be resilient in the face of adversity. Resisting change will only cause you pain. Accepting change by maintaining a positive attitude is crucial. Look for new opportunities to serve others.

The *Golden Rule* suggests that if you would like people to treat you with respect, then you should treat them with respect, too. This old philosophical principle has been formulated in various ways by many different groups throughout history.

People who helped others possess higher positive emotions, lower negative emotions, and have a more profound sense of satisfaction within themselves and their relationships. Compassionate people love to give back even in the smallest ways. They tend to express gratitude, do not emphasize money, are mindful of others, and have higher emotional intelligence. They act on empathy and understand the concept that we are all one.

I don't express feeling bored anymore. I learned that boredom is a state where I can relax and enjoy a break. I have read numerous books on finding a soul mate and twin flames. One, in particular, instructed me to list all aspects I desired and didn't desire in a mate. This included everything from height, weight, hair color, smoking or not, alcohol consumption, likes and dislikes, work ethics, interests, desiring children, and so forth. I discovered that we have many soul mates that venture into and out of our lives. From my understanding, a soul mate is someone who has agreed to enter our lives for a particular amount of time. As both teachers and students to one another, this soul contracted with us (before we entered into these bodies) to assist with an opportunity to learn a valuable lesson for soul growth progression in this lifetime and vice versa. For example, "I will meet with you when you are forty-five and encourage your soul to find more love for yourself." Or, "I will be your child, parent, or friend." The lessons will always be about love. Either loving yourself or finding love in others.

In my search for a partner to share life with, I found a soul mate who confronted his childhood issues of abandonment and abuse. Adopted at birth and later placed in an orphanage, he is now a recovering alcoholic and drug addict. Before his liver transplant, he made his peace with God as he faced possible death. This man possesses the spiritual depth I was searching for. We experienced many months of adjustment at the beginning of our relationship as our inner children triggered each other immensely, providing each of us with opportunities to parent them. With a mutual realization of the work and commitment it takes for a successful relationship, we made it work for both of us. This man is my best friend. He understands, loves, and supports me more than anyone else. As the years increased, the progression of our love has been a wondrous and spiritual journey. I know that our souls have met before and will meet again.

The love within us is meant to extend outward. The closer we grow to our inner light; we feel a natural desire to share it. We long for meaningful work, some creative endeavor that will flow out of us to heal the world. By writing and publishing my books, that is my desire.

"Learn how to express love to others. Let others feel your love by your words, your body language, your attitude, the look in your eyes, your behavior, and your actions. Not only will you touch the lives of thousands of people, but you, yourself, will have greater joy and harmony inside of you than you have ever felt before." - Nick Bunick, *In God's Truth*

Happiness is something that is felt inside of us. It is an emotional state characterized by feelings of joy, excitement, gratitude, pride, optimism, satisfaction, contentment, and fulfillment. Specific thoughts and experiences activate the chemicals dopamine, oxytocin, serotonin, and endorphins in the brain that affect this emotion.

Being happy can have different meanings for different people. Happiness is not a state of ecstasy but rather a state of contentment. It is the feeling we get when we are generous; when we love, create, and appreciate the beauty in nature. Happy people can handle stress better, are healthier, engage in exercise, and eat healthy foods. Pursuing goals and enjoying adventures will bring more significant and long-lasting happiness rather than money, material possessions, or prestige. Being popular or extroverted is not necessary for true happiness. Quality is more important than quantity regarding having just a few close and trusted friends.

Everyone experiences negative and positive emotions, but happy people feel more positive emotions, possessing more satisfaction in their lives. They smile more, complain less, and appear more cheerful. When faced with discomfort, they have a sense of optimism that things will improve.

Some people just seem to be happier, but there are actual methods to develop your happiness. When negative emotions such as pessimism, resentment, and anger are removed, empathy, serenity, and gratitude can take their place, creating happiness in your life. Happiness can be acquired by focusing on gratitude, setting goals for personal growth, volunteering, and being of service to others. Reconstruct your negative thoughts into positive ones, using self-talk and affirmations. Pay attention to your relationships and make some effort in reaching out to others.

You do not need others' approval to be happy. Your happiness is your responsibility, but maintaining it requires nurturing and nourishment. Happiness is a skill that you build for yourself by making positive daily choices. Here are some of the many ways that you can find more happiness in your life:

- Build your self-confidence

- Do the things you love
- Listen to music, sing, and dance
- Celebrate small successes
- Keep a journal of experiences or people that make you happy
- Spend more time with family and friends
- Perform random acts of kindness
- Spend your money on experiences rather than material things
- Play with your pets
- Have more sex
- Go for a walk or exercise
- Sleep longer or take a nap
- Watch a funny movie
- Hang out with people who make you feel happy

Focus on creating the kind of life and relationships you desire, and you will naturally bring fulfillment, satisfaction, and happiness into your life. Happiness is when we're at peace with what we think, say, and do. On your journey, you can find joy in becoming what you dream of being. Some believe that when they buy or pay off a house, lose fifty pounds, or receive a promotion, they will be happy. You don't need to postpone your happiness. You can be happy now. To grow and expand, you must be willing to let go of your limiting beliefs, harmful habits, and negative self-talk. Everyone has the right to be happy no matter what you have done in the past or whatever you may have lost. Millions have turned their lives around finding happiness, and so can you. The only one holding you back from reaching your potential is you.

We are never done learning until we take that last breath. During the pandemic, I realized at a deeper level that we are all one and, in this life, together. I don't take anything for granted anymore and appreciate everything and everyone in my life. When my husband and I camped during the pandemic, I discovered immense pleasure in feeding the squirrels peanut butter and watching them eat. They arrived every morning for feeding, and we all became friends. These are the simple joys in life.

Life is easier for me when I stay in the present moment because who knows what tomorrow will bring? The news constantly changes from day to day with new challenges and surprising statistics. It didn't take long to adjust to not working anymore, as I love not having a particular bedtime or commitments the next day. I understood that life is not about *doing* as much as it is about *being*.

Spread your joy, wisdom, and love. Be an example to all. Give from your heart, sharing your time with others and your children. New research reveals that modern technology is ruining families' quality time together. Gadgets get in the way of families spending time together. Eighty-six percent of parents admit there are times when everyone is at home, but separately watching TV or playing on their phones or computers. Make dinner time family time. Dinner time is a beautiful way for families to spend time together, checking in with each other and hearing about everyone's day. Riding in the car together is another time for family conversation. Today, almost all the chattering is gone, thanks to phones, video games, streaming movies on tablets, and wireless headphones.

Send a note, text, call, or email someone you have not contacted for a while. Wave to your neighbor, buy a friend lunch, or visit someone. Create memories because all you leave behind is love, and that is what others will remember you for.

The world can be a cruel, cold, and ruthless place for those in unfortunate circumstances. People who seem cruel and unkind to themselves may be fighting a battle we can't even imagine. They may be filled with stress and anger and have nothing inside to give to others at this time in their lives. Offer a smile and say a silent prayer for them to move through their difficult situation with the hope of growing into someone better. Attempt to be kind, even when dealing with people who don't seem to deserve it.

The essence of who you are is love, pure love. This is your highest vibration. When you connect with this deepest part of you, you are connecting to God, for *God is Love.*

Enjoy the journey and initiate a life worth living. The power and courage are within you. Ask how you can change yourself to contribute to this world and leave it in a better state than when you arrived. We set our limits in life by choosing to see the world through the eyes of a wondrous child or as a never-ending journey of conflict, obstacles, and misfortunes.

After all, this is the adventure you signed up for!

CHAPTER 11

PURIFYING THE SELF

"Healing doesn't mean the damage never existed.
It means the damage no longer controls our lives."
- Shah Rukh Khan

Our childhood experiences influence aspects of our adult well-being in health, friendships, and even in our capabilities. Some say that "the past is the past", but the past is all too often still alive, continuing to make our world feel unsafe. Trauma is a fact of life. Veterans have to deal with the painful consequences and memories of combat; one in five Americans have been sexually abused; one in four grew up with addicted parents; one in three couples have dealt with physical violence. Everyone reacts to trauma in different ways.

There are many reasons some of us carry emotional wounds from our childhood. Damage from being physically or sexually abused is quite apparent. But there are many kinds of childhood oppression that you might not identify as trauma at all. Trauma can be neglect, the loss of a parent, serious childhood illness, a learning disability, too many siblings, emotionally unavailable or anxious parents, racism, or bullying.

"By age 16, more than two-thirds of children report experiencing at least one traumatic event. A traumatic event poses a threat to a child's life or physical safety. This includes events that are frightening, dangerous, or violent." - Substance Abuse and Mental Health Services Administration (SAMHSA). Those who suffer from unresolved childhood trauma may look normal on the outside, but on the inside, there is a scared, lost child longing for the love, and support they never received. Children who experience trauma are filled with shame, guilt, and low self-esteem.

"There are wounds that never show on the body that are deeper and more hurtful than anything that bleeds." - Laurell K. Hamilton, *Mistral's Kiss*

Experiencing childhood sufferings and losses changes a child forever and can burden them for decades. When hearts have been wounded in early developmental stages, it is easy to put up walls. Healing the harms and injuries of childhood is not a pleasant task to do, but necessary if we want to create the life we want. We start by bravely acknowledging the trauma and taking one step at a time. I compare this process to the grief process, which includes denial, anger, understanding, acceptance, and finally forgiveness.

The effects of being bullied are heartbreaking and can last a lifetime. Bullying can include tripping, hitting, spitting, teasing, name-calling, threats, or spreading rumors and lies about someone. Victims can suffer emotionally, feeling angry, bitter, vulnerable, helpless, frustrated, lonely, and isolated. In adulthood, they may continue to struggle with self-esteem, have difficulty with relationships, and avoid social interactions. They may also have a hard time trusting people and how they view themselves. Physically, they may experience stomach aches and headaches. Two of the first signs that a child is being bullied are slipping grades or skipping school. They may resort to drugs and alcohol, develop depression, or even consider suicide.

Victims may fight back with extreme and sudden violence. *Stopbullying.gov* reports that in twelve of the fifteen school shootings, the shooters had been bullied. According to the Pew Research Center, "59% of U.S. teens have been bullied or harassed online, and a similar share state it's a major problem for people their age. At the same time, teens mostly think teachers, social media companies, and politicians are failing to address this issue." If you see someone being bullied, please stop and act or report it.

"The people who are bullying you, they're insecure about who they are and that's why they're bullying you. It never has to do with the person they're bullying. They desperately want to be loved and accepted and they go out of their way to make people feel unaccepted so that they're not alone." - Madalaine Petsch

Perhaps you carry pain from being criticized, feeling neglected, not feeling heard or appreciated, or feeling like no one loved or cared about you. It could be that you had to take care of the other children and perform most of the household chores. If your emotional and physical needs did not come first, you experienced neglect. I heard the phrase, "Children should be seen and not heard," a hundred times as a child. The effects of waiting and longing to have your feelings heard can last a lifetime.

If you walk on eggshells with someone quick to anger, feel overlooked, or withdraw from others, the problems you had as a child could be affecting you now as an adult. All of us are influenced by memories and experiences we may not remember or don't fully understand. These negative experiences can trigger us, especially when stressed, keeping us from a life we desire. A sense of fear and hopelessness can carry into adulthood. Experiencing trauma can cause us to split from our true selves, and we become our own enemy. We feel unacceptable, unsafe, and spend vast amounts of energy trying to feel anything but the nothingness inside. Behaviors can become irresponsible and high risk, and sometimes we will do anything to get away from our pain. The only way out is through.

Your childhood trauma also lives on in your symptoms. These can include:

- Shock, denial, or disbelief.
- Worry, confusion, and difficulty concentrating.
- Anger, irritability, mood swings, and panic attacks.
- Anxiety, fear, obsessing, or panic attacks.
- Guilt, shame, self-blame, and eating disorders.
- Withdrawing from others and relationship fears.
- Feeling sad, hopeless, and depressed.
- Feeling disconnected or numb.

You might have difficulty trusting others, low self-esteem, the fear of being judged, a need to please others, outbursts of anger and frustration, or social anxiety.

Seeking help displays bravery, enormous courage, and self-love, and is *always* worth the effort. To change something, you must first be aware of it and how it impacts you. Many victims of abuse feel somehow responsible for what they endured. Like me, many minimized their abuse, realizing that others had it much worse. But if it is affecting your ability to experience happiness and peace in your life, it matters.

"Jesus said, 'If you bring forth what is within you, what you bring forth will save you. If you do not bring forth what is within you, what you do not bring forth will destroy you." - Gnostic Gospel of Thomas

The good news is that the effects of abuse *can be* reversed. It is possible to recover and live a meaningful and rewarding life. In John Bradshaw's book, *The Family (*A New Way of Creating Solid Self-Esteem), John shows you ways to escape the oppression of family-reinforced behavior traps from addiction, co-dependency, loss of self-control, and denial. He explains how to make conscious choices that will transform your life. In healing yourself, you heal your family and the world in which you live.

The *CDC* (Kaiser Permanente Adverse Childhood Experiences Study) provides an insightful shift in understanding why humans behave the way we do. *ACE's* science researches the significance and consequences of adverse childhood experiences and what to do to prevent them. Utilizing understanding, nurturing, and healing practices instead of blaming, shaming, and punishing has produced remarkable results with unhealthy and criminal behaviors.

"Trauma is personal. It does not disappear if it is not validated. When it is ignored or invalidated the silent screams continue internally heard by the one held captive. When someone enters the pain and hears the screams, healing can begin." - Danielle Bernock

Childhood trauma can be healed with a trained therapist. Ask your doctor, family, friends, and other healthcare providers for recommendations and create a list of potential therapists. Check their training, skills, and experience and read patient reviews. You can research counselors' credentials and expertise on *healthgrades.com.* Some counselors specialize in particular conditions with specific training in certain fields. A therapist's job is to determine the best method for you with your input and agreement.

Choose a counselor who is covered by your insurance plan and check your out-of-pocket expenses for visits. Your counselor's gender may be important as you will need to openly discuss personal information. The traumatized child that still lives inside you has to feel safe, seen, valued, and heard. It is essential to find a counselor who listens deeply and compassionately, who will consider your treatment preferences, as well as respect your decision-making process. Remember, your therapist is not there to be your friend.

BetterHelp's (*betterhelp.com*) mission is "to make professional therapy accessible, affordable, and convenient so anyone who struggles with life's challenges can get help, anytime and anywhere." It begins with taking a quiz and then getting matched with a licensed professional receiving support via phone or video sessions.

Talk therapy is a traditional approach to healing from trauma and an effective one. You may be asked some hard questions and be challenged. Or, they may invite you to see things from a different perspective. You can let go of all that you may have been holding on to or obsessing about for years by talking about your past. Giving it away to others lessens the impact it has on you. This therapy can be time-consuming and expensive.

Cognitive Processing Therapy (CPT) has effectively reduced symptoms of PTSD, combat, child abuse, rape, and natural disasters. CPT has been shown to reduce the effects of trauma people have experienced as children and adults. CPT focuses on reinterpreting traumatic events experienced by the person creating a new understanding. Twelve sessions are delivered (individually or in instructed group sessions), beginning with an impact statement of understanding why the event happened and beliefs associated with it. After writing a detailed account of the experience, the person reads it aloud in the next session. The therapist uses Socratic questioning, helping the patient develop strategies to operate outside treatment. Patients will be given out-of-session practice assignments.

CBT (Cognitive Behavioral Therapy) is a type of talk therapy that focuses on changing the way you think and behave. This type of therapist will focus on what is going on in the person's current life, rather than what has led up to their problems. The goal is to move forward in time and develop more effective ways of coping with life.

EFT (Emotional Freedom Technique) is a form of acupuncture with no needles. To begin, the issue or problem is identified, and the emotion is uncovered. The intensity of the emotion is given a number from 0-10. This is called (SUDS) the Subjective Units of Distress Scale. A phrase is then designed to acknowledge the problem with how you accept yourself despite it. This wording is an essential part of the process because it tells our system what we are working on. This, in turn, creates energy disruptions in your system so the negative can be neutralized with tapping.

Fingertips are used to tap and stimulate specific energy points on the body. Signals are sent to parts of the brain that control stress and emotion. This energy flows through the body restoring balance to the body's energy system. In restoring this balance, past painful emotions caused by a difficult experience or negative experience are relieved. While concentrating on accepting and resolving negative emotions, tapping on these points accesses your body's natural energy, restoring it to a balanced state. After a round of tapping, the emotions' intensity is compared and measured for progress. When a very traumatic and emotional situation is addressed, this will be the final time you will have to experience the pain associated with the incident. The memory will remain and magically, the emotional pain will disappear.

With EMDR (Eye Movement Desensitization and Reprocessing) you will be asked to focus on a negative thought and your therapist will have you perform specific eye movements simultaneously. The eye movements in EMDR create a calming effect by diverting your attention to the problem. The nervous system relaxes and when the incident is recalled the brain has returned to some type of equilibrium and the incident can be recalled without distress.

EMDR and EFT are processes that require less talking and can plow through issues. Both are similar and healing is quicker and less expensive. With both, you will retain the memory without the troubling emotion that accompanied it before. Another benefit is that these two techniques do not require repeated in-depth discussions of the traumatic event.

Hypnotherapy is a form of psychotherapy. It is sometimes used during counseling to relax a client. When in a hypnotic state, one can openly and safely explore painful, traumatic, and repressed memories that tend to be obscured by the conscious mind. The memory's power of hurting you is removed, allowing you to live without the burden of the trauma. It is a very effective way of accessing the subconscious and visiting the inner child who longs to be heard. Under hypnosis, an individual becomes more open to the hypnotherapist's suggestions and guidance and can make positive changes in his life. Hypnotherapy has been proven effective in the treatment of addiction for some individuals. But the objective of hypnotherapy is to help individuals develop a deeper understanding of themselves.

If you decide not to go the professional route, you can take active steps on your own. There are a lot of factors to consider whether or not to confront abusers. If the parents, family members, or offenders are still alive, you may want to consider talking to them about your past. Share your feelings, but keep in mind that you are looking for validation and closure. Blame and anger will not help the situation. Bring along someone who will support you. The motive for any type of confrontation should be for self-healing. The benefits of confrontation include increases in personal power, assertiveness, self-esteem, with decreases in guilt, depression, helplessness, and fear. Do not expect the abuser to accept responsibility for their actions; in fact, they will probably deny it. Survivors of abuse are sometimes concerned with hurting the abuser's feelings. That fear stems from being trained to submit to adults as children and considering their feelings and not our own. As an adult, you can now be assertive and set boundaries for yourself.

When you confront your abuser face to face, spend some time writing down what you want to say. Make a list of everything you wish to express and practice saying it before the meeting. You may want to ask them just to listen and not talk until you are finished. Let them know how this abuse made you feel and how it affected your life. It may feel like you did not accomplish anything after, but you finally broke that code of silence. You have spoken your truth.

Or you may also consider writing a long letter or email with the same purpose and attitude. A letter or email gives you the time to think out your thoughts, giving the other person time to digest what you are saying and the ability to read it again and again for understanding. If the other person has passed away, you can write a letter and read it to their spirit. I talked with my father on the other side with and through a medium. The results were unexpectedly remarkable. You can also write a letter with no intention of sending it. Read it out loud to yourself or someone else and then burn and bury it. I like to ask the Universe to transform the smoke into positive energy and send it to someone who needs it the most at that time.

Journaling is an excellent tool for releasing emotions, thoughts, tensions, and feelings. It helps you uncover insights from deep within your subconscious. This kind of therapy enables the person to gain clarity, validate experiences, and develop a deeper understanding of themselves and situations. Studies show the emotional and physical health benefits of writing and allowing your thoughts to flow, releasing unwanted thoughts and feelings. It helps you connect to your most authentic and deepest self, increasing awareness and insight, thereby accelerating the healing process. If you have trouble expressing your thoughts to a therapist, sharing your journal can be a communication tool. You can choose to write at a specific time every day or keep your journal and a pen handy, writing down your thoughts and feelings when they arise. Worrisome thoughts released from the mind no longer take up space, making room for positive thoughts. You can include in the journal things you are worried about, how your day went, what you are grateful for, feelings, struggles, talking with your angels or those on the other side, or whatever comes to mind. Purchase a new beautiful journal and fancy pen that will keep you motivated to write every day to keep you on your healing journey.

There have been numerous studies in medical and psychological publications which conclude that prayer and meditation influence our state of mind, thereby affecting our bodies. Studies have indicated that people who engage in this effort regularly have changes in their frontal lobes, the part of the brain which controls concentration and focus. Frontal lobes are connected to motor function, problem solving, memory, language, judgment, impulse control, rationality, and social behavior.

In religions, prayers are directed to God. In more mystical traditions, prayer is focused inside the self, where our divinity resides. Eastern traditions focus on the word "meditation" rather than the word "prayer." Prayer can influence our thinking, aids in processing emotions, and releases them. No matter which form of prayer you use, the more self-aware you are, the more effective it will be. We can let go and give it to the all-intelligent God/Universe and feel connected to something bigger than ourselves.

Affirmative prayer involves connecting with the spirit of God within us, and affirming positive beliefs about the desired outcome. We believe that each of us is being led to our highest good as we give thanks in advance. We don't always know what is best for us, so we trust the Universe will provide accordingly. Affirmative prayer is the same manner of prayer Jesus taught when he said, "And so I tell you, whatever you ask for in prayer, believe that you have received it, and it will be yours," (Mark 11:24). With this type of summoning, we act as if we have already received the results we were asking for. An example would be to say, "Thank you for sending me the partner who is right for me," instead of saying, "Please God, send me a soulmate."

Metaphysics teaches us that our thoughts transmit magnetic energy, and this energy attracts other energies on the same frequency. Like attracts like. Conscious or not, your thoughts are sending energy that is attracting more of the same. When you remain focused on your intentions, you will draw those things into your life. This is the power of prayer.

" Affirmative prayer sets into motion the forces that enable us to manifest what we pray for. Prayer is ineffective when it is accompanied or followed by negative thinking, or the endless repeating of affirmations. We have to put power and intensity into our thought, change our thought, and believe in the guidance we are receiving." - Rosemary Ellen Guiley, *Prayer Works*

Rituals have been around for a long time and are highly effective in letting go of things that no longer serve you. A ritual is an act or ceremony that helps you gain a sense of control and purpose. When letting go of something, you make room for the new. The use of water offers an opportunity to immerse and cleanse and is used in religious and ceremonial traditions such as christenings, baptisms, and initiations. Using water literally washes hands of unwanted problems, thoughts, and feelings. Set your intention using an affirmation such as, "I wash my hands of this person or problem." You may use salt in the ceremony as water and salt are known to be energetically cleansing substances. Rock salt is known as halite and is derived from a crystal. Crystals can transform dense and unpleasant energies into more useful, harmless energies. You can also use sea salt or Pink Himalayan salts as they are natural and pure energetically. But in a pinch, table salt will do.

Unity Church performs a burning bowl ceremony at the beginning of each new year. This type of ceremony is a powerful way to remove old patterns from your life. After recalling something you want to release, write it down on a piece of paper. It can be old wounds, worries, a person, habits, or negative thought patterns. Fire is a symbol of purification, wisdom, passion, and knowledge. Light a fire in a pot, fireplace, or bowl, dropping your paper into it. As you watch the smoke rise, visualize your statement of release traveling into the smoke. You may say an affirmation such as, "I release myself, as I let go of this burden." Or, "I release you and let God be in charge." Remove the ashes from your property, bury them somewhere, or put them into a lake or body of water. This ceremony can be performed at your home, alone, or at a gathering with others.

Self-help books have helped millions of people transform their lives by building awareness, providing information, and teaching important skills. Many of the books that were highly instrumental in my transformation are mentioned or quoted throughout this book.

Crying facilitates healing and is a sign of courage, strength, and authenticity. Researchers state that crying is good for sadness and stress. Emotional tears contain high levels of the stress hormones oxytocin and endorphins, which are our body's natural pain killers. These chemicals help ease physical and emotional pain, making us feel better and healing our hearts. We can have breakthroughs when we allow ourselves to finally feel the pain and open those flood gates releasing what has been held inside us for so long. Let the males in your life know that it's ok to cry.

Here is another self-motivated process you can use for self-healing. This technique reminds me of EFT without tapping. Locate a quiet place where you won't be disturbed. Sit comfortably with your eyes closed, and take several deep breaths, bringing awareness into your body. Think of a situation that you've been upset about recently. Review what happened in as much detail as possible, imagining yourself back in that time and place. Experience it all again with your senses. What emotions are you feeling? Unresolved traumas remain stored in our bodies until they are released. The symptoms we feel, are a clue to where that trauma has been stored. When stress gets released from our bodies, physical symptoms can be significantly reduced or completely gone.

Next, mentally scan your body for any sensations. Observe any physical response you experience, such as tingling, tightness, burning, or pain. Associate an emotion with each of the feelings you feel. Is the tightness in your chest anxiety? Is the pain in your neck anger? Fully accept what you feel, saying," It is OK for me to be feeling this anger, sadness, depression, etc." Do this with every emotion you feel and accept your humanness by saying," I love myself for this (emotion)." Don't try to change your feelings or hide from them. Acknowledge and welcome any discomfort you feel, knowing it will help you to heal.

Let your body respond the way it wants or needs to by crying, yelling, or punching something. Ask yourself, "If this sensation or emotion could talk to me, what would it say?"

Write out the answers to this question and what you experienced for ten minutes without stopping. Talking or writing about your experiences and emotions is an essential step in the healing process. Again, writing letters to those who hurt you can be an effective method for moving a feeling out of your consciousness. Visualize the energy your emotional suffering took up inside you leaving your body or perform a ritual of physical release, like burning a letter you've written to the person who hurt you. I like to imagine depositing the negative released energy into a helium balloon, releasing it into the sky until it disappears from my sight.

Transformation is attained by taking baby steps. Each baby step is significant as we cannot accomplish a task without one step leading to the next. Going slow will rewire your brain, building your self-confidence as you methodically release the pain associated with the memories. When it is gone, it is gone forever, especially with EFT and EMDR. The memories will remain, but the feelings that were attached to them will vanish.

If you have a loved one who has suffered emotional suffering, your support is crucial. Most importantly, be patient and understanding without judgment. The healing journey takes time. Be there to talk and listen without forcing them to talk about something they are not ready to discuss. Try to remember the second agreement and don't take their anger personally. Validate their feelings and emotions by providing understanding and empathy. Empower them by letting them know that they can let go of being the victim, becoming the victor.

There are many benefits for trauma survivors to join a group in addition to individual therapy. There are several types of groups that offer help for a wide variety of conditions such as depression, ADHD, eating disorders, PTSD, phobias, substance disorders, etc. Seek support groups at hospitals, mental health clinics, private practices, and community centers. People who are in similar situations can offer support, validation, confidence, and encouragement. Sharing your story with others can be very healing. One of the most important benefits is learning that there are others like you who are suffering from the same condition.

Many tests and quizzes are available online that can measure your impact on childhood oppression. One is the ACE (*Adverse Childhood Experience*) quiz. The test consists of ten questions and is easy and quick to take. If you are interested in taking the test, the link is *https://acestoohigh.com/got-your-ace-score/*.

Highly sensitive people are more likely to feel all things deeply. If you've been told that you're "too sensitive" or that you "shouldn't think so much," you may be what is known as a highly sensitive person or HSP. Violent movies, noisy crowds, bright lights, hunger, and uncomfortable clothing can make you feel very tense and irritable. HSP are moved deeply by nature, art, and the human spirit, owning a complex inner life with strong feelings and deep thoughts. Highly sensitive people are thought to make up roughly

20% of the general population. They are considered to have particular genetic characteristics with an increased central nervous system. HSP tend to get more stressed when faced with a difficult situation and are easily offended. In my case, it also produces insomnia. Empaths feel the loss of a relationship more intensely and engage in rumination and self-doubt and pick up others' needs and feelings. It can help to add more positivity to your life, avoid stressors, learn to say no, and allow your home to be your sanctuary when feeling overwhelmed. Here is a quiz that can help you determine whether you share this trait. If you want to take the test you can find it at *https://hsperson.com/test/highly-sensitive-test/*.

Narcissistic parents are self-focused and cannot make themselves available to others as they are incapable of love and compassion. For children, this impact is very painful and ongoing in their lives. Children raised in a narcissistic family have a history of complex trauma, experience emotional flashbacks, are highly sensitive, and possess exaggerated behaviors. If you were raised by (or are being raised by) a narcissistic parent, there is a support group online for you. Here you can share your stories, questions, histories, triggers, thoughts, fears, and triumphs. Check this out at *https://www.reddit.com/r/raisedbynarcissists*.

Inner child work helps you build a strong relationship with yourself. There are many workbooks out there, but I recommend *Homecoming* by John Bradshaw. This book enables you to connect with your child through each developmental stage. There are questionnaires to help you understand how your child was wounded and how it affects your adult life.

You can also help heal your inner child and the world by raising your children with a commitment to giving them what they need, attempting to not repeat the past. Many healed adults have continued self-healing by helping less fortunate children, participating in teaching, coaching, mentoring, volunteering, or by becoming a therapist. Above all, do not isolate yourself. Connect with others by volunteering, participating in social activities, or joining a support group for trauma survivors. If there isn't one in your area, start one. Helping others benefits our mental health and well-being. It reduces stress and improves mood, self-esteem, and happiness.

When you improve your skills, habits and revaluate yourself, you gain a deeper understanding of others and the world. One reason people don't receive what they desire is simply that they give up too soon. Success does not come as quickly as we would like it to. We tend to want things right now. Persistence and patience are key. The space that the discomfort took up inside of you can now be filled with more positive energy and create a life that you deserve and love. You deserve it and you are worth it!

"My mother gave birth to the child I was, but it was me who gave birth to the man I am today." - Namrata Gupta

Choices are the decisions we make and the actions we take. You can let life happen, blowing like a leaf in the wind, or make choices to create the life you desire. As children, our parents made choices for us, but we have control over what we think, say, and do as adults. The personal choices we make every day shape us into being who we are and how others see us. Choosing what is important to you is what makes you independent and in charge of your own life. Know that you can accept things as they exist, or live consciously, accepting your responsibility for changing them.

"I honor the place within you where the entire Universe resides; I honor the place within you of love, of light, of truth, of peace; I honor the place within you, where, when you are in that place in you, and I am in that place in me, there is only one of us."

Namaste!

ABOUT THE AUTHOR

Mary M Betsworth cherishes her time spent with her loving husband, children, grandchildren, and Coco. She enjoys writing, healing others, gardening, exploring mountains, camping, and teaching.

The author is an ordained minister, Reiki/Seikim Master, certified Emotional Freedom Technique practitioner, and resides with her husband, Richard, in Omaha, Nebraska.